Ben & Bonita,

Your faith is an
example to all,
especially me.

This book belongs to:

Mr. William B. Woolard

How to Manage Money Like a Minister:

The A, B, C's of Pinching Pennies Like a Pastor

By

Dr. Michael F. Price

Running Angel Books

Published by Second Wind Publishing

Kernersville

Running Angel Books
Second Wind Publishing, LLC
931-B South Main Street, Box 145
Kernersville, NC 27284

This book is a work of non-fiction. All ideas, statements, and
insights are solely the work of the author.

First Running Angel Books edition published June, 2010.
Running Angel Books, Running Angel, and all production
design are trademarks of Second Wind Publishing, used
under license.

For information regarding bulk purchases of this book,
digital purchase and special discounts, please contact the
publisher at www.secondwindpublishing.com

Front cover design by Danielle Rees

Manufactured in the United States of America
ISBN 978-1-935171-34-8

Acknowledgements

Thomas A. Edison was correct when he said nearly 80-years ago, *"genius is one percent inspiration and ninety-nine percent perspiration."* To be the best one can be physically, intellectually, or spiritually, requires hard work and devotion. It requires not weeks or months but years and years of tireless effort and commitment. Edison should know since most would agree that he had more disappointments than achievements.

Far be it for me to profess to be a genius...or a financial know-it-all author for that fact. After all, I graduated in the bottom 25% of my high school class (110th out of 143). Ask any of my teachers and they will tell you: it took a great deal of perspiration my last year of high school just so I could walk across the stage with the rest of the Class of 1973 of Magnolia High School! Accordingly, Edison's epic quote does *not* seem to fit my life. If anything, the opposite could be said. I am where I am because of ninety-nine percent inspiration and one percent perspiration.

And it is to the countless individuals that gave me the inspiration...the push...that I dedicate this work. Some of these individuals are deceased and some are still inspiring me daily by their faith, their work ethic, and their general sense of stewardship and money management. In their own loving way, each contributed to this work.

To my mother, Mary Lou, who by word and deed put our needs above her wants and saw to it that my three brothers and two sisters had like everybody else. My mother knew the importance of saving for those unexpected situations, the emotional lift that came when she could splurge for a special occasion like a birthday, and the sheer joy that came from feeding the members of my college baseball team when we stopped by unexpectedly after a game. Living more with less so that others could have was not a temporary approach to life for her...it was a way of life.

To my three brothers (Frank, Rodney, and David) and two sisters (Cheryl and Melissia) who continue this tradition today. Like our mother, they know the value of hard work and the emotional and financial rewards that hard work brings with it. Above all, they know it's not how one lived their life yesterday that counts. Rather, it's how one lives today and tomorrow that will leave the biggest footprint.

As well, my thankful appreciation extends to all the countless individuals in the churches that I have had the honor of serving the past one-score and five years. Thank you for your inspiration and your example: First Christian Church, Bossier City, Louisiana; First Christian Church, Baton Rouge, Louisiana; Smyrna Christian Church,

Bruington, Virginia; St. Paul's Christian Church, Raleigh, North Carolina; and most of all, First Christian Church, Washington, North Carolina. The members and friends of these first four churches provided me some of the inspiration and example to write this work, but it was the members and friends of the last church, FCC, Washington, that supplied me the inspiration, the example, and the time to write this book. Thank you to all.

Lest I forget, I want to extend a gentle smile and a heartfelt thanks to all those that had a part in helping this work come to fruition, including the proofreaders (Bobby Alligood, Mary Alice Chapin, and Bob and Betty Cook), the cover-designer and graphic person, Danielle Rees, and Dr. Mike Simpson and the good folks at Second Wind Publishing. Still, I would be amiss if I did not mention the crucial role that Rev. Sue Halford played in all of this. After all, she was the one that put me in touch with Mike and Second Wind Publishing.

Above all, I acknowledge with love the role that my dear wife, Betty, played in getting this book from my head to your hands. Truly, she may be the biggest inspiration next to my mother. Maybe it was Betty's upbringing (she, too, was raised by a single mother), maybe it was her education (did I mention that she is a CPA with an MBA in Accounting), or maybe it was her broad experience in the workplace with some of the most noted companies in North Carolina. Whatever the case, Betty has to be one of the smartest money-people that I have ever known! Or, it may have been her way of inspiring me to write when I could have been doing something else during my sabbatical last year. Even to this day, I remember her *words of inspiration* as she left for work each morning during the summer of 2009. "I'll be home around 6:30pm," she would say, "and I expect to see some words of wisdom on your laptop!"

To all then, for your inspiration, I acknowledge your place in the pages that follow. You told me I could and you showed me I should write this book. I only hope that this work inspires you as much as you have inspired me.

— ***Dr. Michael F. Price***

Contents

Introduction

If I were to follow the lead of former President Richard M. Nixon and tell you that I was "born in the house my father built", I would *not* be totally honest. In fact, it would be an outright lie.

To begin, I was born in a hospital--Wetzel County Hospital located in New Martinsville, West Virginia--to be exact. I'm not sure when my mother went into labor, the exact time of my birth, or even what the weather conditions were like on January 6, 1955. What I do know is that I came into this world on a Thursday, and I weighed 6 pounds and 13 ounces. I know this because of that trusty piece of paper known as a birth certificate. When Dr. Hornbrook slapped my behind and gave me my first breath I became the fourth of my mother's children. Waiting for her to return home from the hospital were my sister who is 8-years older than me, a brother 7-years older, and another brother 3-years older. Between that day in January and five years hence, my three siblings and I would be joined by two more kids...another sister and another brother.

As well, it would be difficult to follow the lead of Pres. Nixon because the first house I remember us living in was not what one might call a house. Today, it would be called a garage apartment since it was located above a two-car garage on

Clark Street. I'm not sure whom my mother rented from, how much the monthly rent was, or the square feet of that apartment. However, I remember it was a small place, located at the end of a driveway, and bordered the railroad tracks. More vivid are the memories I have of my mother rushing down the two dozen steps or so when she heard the whistle of an approaching coal-burning train. In quick time, she had to take those freshly washed clothes off the line lest they be covered in soot!

Above all, it wouldn't be right to tell you that I was born in the house that my father built because of something I discovered several years later. Granted, my mother's name appeared on the birth certificate right where it should be, but the line where my father's name should have appeared was blank! Why?

For one, my father may not have been around on that day in January, 1955. It seems that in the two decades that followed his honorable discharge from the U.S. Marines in 1947, he was in-and-out of jail. Not just the local jail, mind you, but the state penitentiary.

His first stop was the county jail on a charge of breaking and entering. He and two of his cohorts were arrested for breaking into the storehouse of the local yacht club. Deciding he had better things to do as he awaited trial, he escaped from the jail. Several months later, he was arrested for burglary at a local wholesale beer distributorship. Among his possessions at the time of the arrest were a revolver, two bottles of whiskey, electric (coffee) percolator and one T-bone steak! In time, he was sent to the state facility where he served nearly five years. One month after his release, he was back in prison for breaking his parole. He was discharged the following year, but within a few months he was back on charges of grand larceny. Inmate number 5590 was finally released (for good) two days before Christmas, 1966.

> *Inmate number 5590 was finally released (for good) two days before Christmas 1966.*

A second and more convincing reason there is no father's name on my birth certificate (or for that fact, my younger sister's as well) is that my mother and my father were not married. Since both are now deceased, it's difficult to ask why they never "tied the knot." They must have loved each other and he must have been around somewhat, because my younger sister "officially" joined the family less than two years after I was born.

Clearly...to say that I was born in the house my father built would *not* be a true statement. I was born in a hospital, to a single-parent, and we lived in a garage apartment that my mother rented.

So what, you may ask, does all of this have to do with money management and personal finance? My answer: *everything*. As people who study other people will tell you, we are the result of our environment. Yes, where and how we grew-up has a great deal of influence on how we go about living our lives. I'm not sure how she did it--emotionally, physically, or financially-- but my single mother raised six children! More, we did not want for much of anything. We always received gifts on Christmas and on our birthdays. Somehow, and I'll never know how, we all got new clothes at the start of each school year. Above all, the refrigerator and the food pantry always seemed to be full. But what is most shocking is that my mother did most of this from the $95.00 a month she received from public assistance! More, she provided for us so that we could live full, regular lives even though she did not have the benefit of child support,

> *...my mother has to be the best money-manager ever!*

3

alimony, or some nest-egg left by her parents. Granted, we got some help from immediate family members on occasion, from several loving people that lived around town, and from my mother washing-and-ironing other people's clothes and cleaning their houses (don't tell the county, state, or federal people they'll want their money back). If I say it once, I'll say it a thousand times: *my mother has to be the best money manager of all time!*

Think about it. When I was born some two-score and fifteen years ago, a dozen eggs cost 78 cents, a loaf of bread was 18 cents, and milk sold for 72 cents a gallon. In addition, average rent was $87.00 a month. Finally, the average annual salary was between $4,100.00 and $5,000.00. As for the

> *...she was able to do so because of her personal approach to stewardship and money management.*

price of gas, it was 29 cents a gallon (this last point would have mattered little, however, because my mother never learned to drive so we didn't have a car). I'm not sure how these prices compare to today's prices, but the fact remains that my single, limited income mother provided for her family. How?

I am fully convinced that my mother was able to do what she did because of her personal approach to stewardship and money management.

First, she fought daily to control her expenses and not the other way around. Granted, she received a monthly check from the state welfare department and it went a long way in helping with the family costs (remember, she received $95.00 a month and a large portion of that went for rent). And yes, others around us helped out as did the meager money she earned from doing other people's laundry and cleaning houses. But when it came down to it, she resisted the temptation to buy something just because it was on sale or because she may have some money left-over at the end of the month (as strange as it sounds, it did happen on occasion). In like manner, she was wise and always did her homework. At any time of the day, it was not uncommon to come home and find my mother combing the flyer of the local newspaper for sales or coupons. Finally, and maybe her most lasting tactic of money management, she used what little money she had left-over from the expense-side and used that on the income-side. Unlike most that would take whatever surplus money is left at the end of the month and buy something, she used the surplus from her expenses to supplement her income. Bottom line: she did not waste a single dime!

Although all of this sounds simple and quite elementary, it's not. For one, setting out on a course toward better stewardship of money entails education, discipline, and commitment. While some *choose* to do it until things get better in their lives, others, like my mother, do it out of *necessity* each and every day. Considering the current economic times, it seems that more and more people are doing it today more for the latter than the former.

However, a more pressing concern is how to even begin such a monumental task. Everybody has their ideas, and the media is filled with financial experts who lead us to believe they have the answers. Trouble is they seem to be far removed from the everyday financial challenges that most Americans face on a regular basis. People want to know how they can reduce their utility bills and not so much about how the major movers in the utilities sector of the stock exchange are doing. People want to know how to live more with the money they have and not so much how to shelter future earnings. I am convinced that the majority of the people in this country today want to know how they can reduce their telephone bill instead of how much the telephone companies are making.

Clearly, what most people are waiting on is a list of *Hints from Heloise* but with a financial slant.

Americans have waited patiently for such a work, but there seems to be nothing out there or anything on the way. In the meantime, the financial challenges continue for most. Wait no longer, my friend, your help has arrived and such a work is here!

In the pages that follow, I lay out what I feel are the best money-saving tips and countless cost-effective ways to cut everyday expenses. From how to go about cutting

> *...Hints from Heloise but with a financial slant.*

costs on auto insurance to cutting educational costs, from what to watch out for when buying items such as clothes to when to buy food at the grocery store, and from knowing when to travel and how to stay for free, they're all found within these pages. More, I place them into 26 simple categories...one for each letter of the alphabet...so that you will not be overwhelmed with so many ideas you'll stop reading after the first chapter. Granted, the length of each category subject varies, but I've endeavored to make these money-tips personal yet void of repetition and over-lap. If these tips happen to sound familiar with something else you may have heard or seen, it's purely coincidental. After all, no one has the market cornered on common sense. Finally, keep in mind this is *not* some "here are some solutions and wait until next issue for more." Rather, this is a timely, comprehensive, and reference work that lays-out in simple terms how to become a better manager of your money via reducing your expenses. The title says it all: *How to Manage Money Like a Minister* (or *The A-B-C's of Pinching Pennies Like a Pastor).*

Still, let me say this: I am not an economist and the grade I received in Economics 101 proves it. My degrees are in history, theology, and education. However, what I may lack in economic and financial theory is made up for in real life, practical, and first-hand knowledge. I am not new to the in's-and-out's of money management, personal finance, and good stewardship. In addition to having the privilege, and I mean that in every sense of the word, to see first-hand how my mother raised six kids on a limited income, I have also been blessed to have been surrounded by people who know how to make the most of the money they had. Yes, I saw how little (financial) supply we had and how big the demand was. During the twenty-four years my mother lived after I was born (she died at the age of 52), I got to see "cost benefit analysis" from a personal perspective as she searched high-and-low for the best bargains. Hey...I guess I do know a little about economics!

However, the expert money management and stewardship that I saw displayed by my mother are not the only aspects that qualify me to write this book. Combined, my own financial challenges before and after a divorce, the stewardship and money management that I've seen displayed among the congregations I've served during my quarter century of parish ministry, and the informal education along the way provide ample background. Truth is...I've had some great teachers.

...a timely, comprehensive, and reference work that lays out in simple terms how to become a better manager of your money...

Allow me to close by saying a few things about practicing good money management in general and this work in particular. As I stated earlier, successful money management and personal finance requires education, discipline, and commitment. It cannot be done overnight or hit-and-miss. To become an educated consumer and a smart-spender requires a change of lifestyle...not a radical one, mind you, that friends and neighbors will think you've gone off the deepend. Rather, I am saying that we need to live our own lives and not worry about what others are saying or doing. Trying to keep-up with the Jones may have gotten us into this current economic predicament in the first place. In these suggestions that I offer (yes, they are just that...suggestions), I ask that you look at them like you do the food when you eat at a cafeteria...take and digest what you want and leave the rest. There are some things that you will like and others you will not. Hey, the bottom line is that I'm not twisting your arm and not everything will work for your particular situation. You may not feel comfortable about

> *...we need to live our own lives and not worry about what others are saying or doing.*

doing a house exchange with a complete stranger from another continent. Again, take what you want and leave the rest.

Next, let me say that I have purposely stayed away from countless financial areas. I did this partly out of respect of not wanting to publish a work that equals *War and Peace* or *Encyclopedia Britannica* in length. As much as possible, I have tried to "get to the point" in this work. You do not need to spend time trying to find advice on how to reduce bank charges. Simply go to the letter "B" and see what I offer.

I am just a regular guy...that wants you to know what I know about stewardship and personal finance.

Finally, I want to go back to what I said earlier about my expertise. Again, I am *not* a financial planner or an expert in the field of money management and personal finance. I am just a regular guy...if a minister can be called a regular guy...that wants you to know what I know about personal finance and stewardship. The things that are *not* covered in this work may very well be the things that you go to an expert to find out about like investments, financing, and tax preparation. Maybe Mark Twain had yours truly in mind when he said that "a little knowledge is a dangerous thing."

That said, here's a great deal (if not all) of what I know about money management, personal finance, and stewardship beginning with the first letter of the alphabet and things involving automobiles...

Automobiles

Again, we never had a car growing up...at least one that I can remember. The first car I do remember sitting in the drive-way was a 1949 Ford which belonged to my oldest brother. Since money was at a minimum, he used it mainly for driving to school, going to work at a local drug store and at the nearby drive-in movie theater on weekends, and making necessary runs here-and-there. My older sister had a purple Corvair convertible, but she did not get that until she had graduated from high school and was out working on her own. As for my other older brother, his first car was a 1964, lime-colored, Plymouth with standard shift on the column. It was on this car that I learned to drive! Sadly, though, it is in that same car that I had my first (and only) accident.

It was around midnight on the 23rd of December, 1971, and I was coming home after visiting a friend. I had just gotten on the four-lane highway that leads back home when the car in front of me suddenly slowed down. Automatically, I passed them. This proved to be a big mistake, because I no sooner was in the passing lane than I was hit head-on by a drunk driver going the wrong way! Thankfully, I was not hurt that bad...a broken right hand, a cut above the bridge of my nose, and a similar cut above my right eye that required several dozen stitches. Sadly, my brother's car was totaled. Come to think of it, he has never let me forget that I wrecked his car!

> *...my brother ...has never let me forget that I wrecked his car!*

My first car was a yellow, late 1960's, Volkswagen "fastback" wagon that I purchased for $500.00. I was 18 years-old at the time. The car didn't last long, though, because the engine blew-up one day as I was driving it. It seems that the car had a serious oil leak that the former owner "forgot" to tell me. In the end, the oil leak, my lack of mechanical expertise, and my devil-may-care attitude proved to be a lethal combination.

My next car was also a Volkswagen...but this time it was a VW Beetle. Although that particular car lasted me through fours-years of college, it met its demise when another teenager from my town rear-ended me at a stop sign. His words following the accident, "I didn't think you were going to stop!"

In the thirty years that have followed, I have had no car, a 1975 Nissan station wagon that I purchased while I was in seminary from a fellow student-minister that moon-lighted as a used car salesman, and four (count them...four) Volvos! Clearly, *Volvo for life*. However, I must add that all of those Volvos were used, and each was between 5 – 7 years old when they were purchased.

And during those last thirty years, I have come to understand a great deal about cars, particularly when to buy them, what to look for when buying them, financing, maintenance, and most of all, how to do all of this in the most economical, yet safest, way.

In this opening chapter, I want to share with you some of the things that I have come to understand about cars. Granted, some of this you may already know and some of the suggestions that follow may be new to you. To help you better understand what I'm suggesting, I have categorized the suggestions into a "before" (things to keep in mind before you buy a car), "during" (things to keep in mind as you meet with a salesperson), and an "after" (things to do after you've made the purchase). Above all, I want to share with you these things to make you a better steward and manager of your personal finances. This chapter may be lengthy, so stay with me.

Before

Do your homework. Know what kind of car you want and begin researching long before you want to buy. Do you want to buy a new one, a used one, or do you want to lease? How long do you plan on driving it? Do you want a car that gets excellent gas mileage or are you looking for a car that's at the top of the list in safety features?

> *Do your homework.*

Personally, I keep a few things in mind when I begin looking to replace an older car with a newer one. First, I never buy new because of the rapid depreciation that follows. Someone once told me that new cars depreciate as much as 30% once you drive them off the lot! Next, I buy with the intent of driving the car as long as I can. The last car I had before the one I'm currently driving was a 1987 Volvo. When it was purchased (again, used) in the mid-1990's it had 55,000 miles on it. By the time I sold it for junk last January, I had driven it an additional 213,000 miles! <u>A simple rule of thumb</u>: when the repair costs get to be more than the car is worth I begin my search. Lastly, I look at the features I want in a car. As a minister in a smaller town, I don't spend that much time in my car. Subsequently, I don't need all the whistles and gadgets. Personally, I want to drive a car that gets moderate gas mileage and is safe to drive.

The internet is filled with websites that compare cars and their features. If you're not near a computer, then go to the magazine section of the closest library and review what *Consumer's Reports* says. Before you even step one-foot into a car dealership, you should know the model of car you want, the accessories, etc. Coming into a car dealer with little or no-idea of these things is asking for problems, headaches, and a heavy dose of frustration. Even worse, you may even end-up making decisions on impulse.

Have a general idea of the price of the car you want. Again, there are countless resources available to you that can offer a "pretty good" idea of how much a specific car with specific options

> **Let them make the first move about the cost of the vehicle.**

costs the dealer including *Kelly Blue Book* and *Edmonds*. To get the best deal, look for the price the dealer paid for the car and not the sticker price. I understand that a good base-line price is 5% – 10% over what the dealer paid for the car. However, don't forget to include into the price of the car some of those standard fees like sales tax, title, registration, and delivery fees.

Time your purchase (if possible) for either the last of the month, the last of the quarter, or the end of the car selling year...September. Generally, car salespeople work on a commission. As the month or quarter (March, June, September, December) draws to a close, some great deals can be made because salespeople need the money and dealers want to move cars. As for waiting until September to purchase a new car, the answer is simple: the next year's models are starting to be shipped to local dealers and the current inventory must go!

During

Know (calculate) beforehand what you're willing to spend and what your budget will allow. In other words, know what you can spend over the financing "life" of the car and do not budge. Knowing what you can spend may take some time to determine since you will need to consider everyday living expenses that you currently have (mortgage or rent, groceries, utilities, etc) and other expenses that may be increased as a result of getting the car (increased car insurance rates, etc), but the effort could save you money in the long run. Although the monthly payments on a car may sound attractive and fit within your budget, I warn you to proceed with caution. Yes, the monthly payments may be less than you calculated, but you could end-up paying more in the long-run in interest! In addition, never, and I mean never, tell the salesperson how much you're planning to spend. If you do, then you give away a great deal of your bargaining power. Let them make the first move about the cost of the vehicle.

Settle on the price of the new car first, then go with whether you will trade-in a car or not. Here, it is crucial to know the difference between trade-in price (the price that the dealer will most likely give you for your car), private price (the price you may get if you sold it yourself) and dealer price (the price most dealers in your area would pay for a similar car including any additional charges they may incur along the way). After settling on the price of the new car, ask the salesperson what they will give you for your old car (trade-in). If the amount is below what you've found doing your research for a similar car with the same options, then give serious thought to selling the car yourself. Remember: you want to begin the process by determining the lowest price that the salesperson will sell you the car. You, then, subtract from that price.

Know what you want (and will pay for) and don't want (and will refuse to pay for) in the way of options. Again, this is where your homework comes in.

From your research, you will have already "pretty much" determined how much adding cruise control, a CD player, a GPS or other accessories to the new car will cost. Some of these options are available separately, but others can only be bought as part of a package. In addition to keeping a running tab as you go and adding these numbers to the base price of the car, remember to negotiate for each (to learn more about how to negotiate, go to the chapter entitled "N: negotiating").

When the salesperson begins to add on those last-minute options, put your foot down.

rust proofing...no, since most, if not all vehicles, are already treated against rust at the factory.

fabric protection...no, like rust proofing, it's usually done at the factory. If not, you can do it yourself by purchasing a can of spray-on protection.

paint sealant...again no, because most auto parts stores carry a do-it-yourself kind that costs tons less and produces the same results.

dealer prep...no, how much does it cost to remove the plastic from the seats, walk around the car and look for scratches, or wash it.

extended warranty...no, enough already!

However, if your salesperson tells you that these things along with a list of other things have already been added and you have no choice but to pay for them, then, in addition to giving them the "I-didn't-fall-off-the-apple-cart-yesterday" look, simply lean on their desk, look at that person with raised eyebrows, and say "I don't care and I'm not paying for them." If that person is smart and wants to keep you as a customer, then they'll say that they're going to throw them in for free. Who said you're no good at negotiating?

> *"I-didn't-fall-off-the-apple-cart-yesterday" look,...*

Bottom line: when it comes time to talk about options and accessories with the salesperson, keep this simple thing in mind. The more accessories on a car, the greater the chance one of them will need repaired. And when it needs repaired or replaced, how much will it cost? The more basic the car...the less it costs to operate it. More, those extras seldom add much, if any, to the resale value of the car when it comes time to sell the car.

If asked about financing, be courteous and hear their side of the story, and if it doesn't fit your particulars, tell the salesperson that you have (will get) your own. At first glance, the zero-down, zero-interest, and zero-payments for the first year sounds good.

Then, the second year comes around and you realize the error of your ways. In addition to your car depreciating nearly 1/3, you still owe all the monthly payments (36 or 48 or whatever)..

Regardless of where you borrow, remember the general rule of thumb when financing a new car: pay 20% down, avoid financing the car for more than four years, and make sure the monthly payments do not exceed 10% of your monthly income.

> *...you're in control and don't forget it!*

Leasing? It matters little, if any, to me what year or model car I'm driving. I'm one of those individuals that does not have to have a new car every 24 – 36 months. What does matter to me is the cost to operate a car on the road, the car's dependability, and if that car is safe. Leasing? It's not for me. My last car was a 1987, and when it was retired the odometer indicated 268,000 miles. My current car has 125,000 on it, and I plan to drive it until it drops. Leasing? It's definitely not for me!

Remember, all the stars have to line-up for you when buying a new car. If you're not especially impressed with a certain year or model of car, then wait. If you're not happy with what the salesperson is offering in the way of accessories or options, then walk away. If the financing of that new car puts undue stress on your regular budget, then maybe you should put off purchasing until a later date. Like most other things in life, you're in control and don't you forget it!

After

If you happened to buy a new car or purchased a used one, it's not only important to make sure you're getting a reliable car but just as crucial to keep that car in tip-top shape. After all, we want it to last, and getting the car to last involves doing regular things to that car that may extend its life. What are those things that we need to do? I'm glad you asked. In the paragraphs that follow, I have listed several "car things" that you can do that will not only keep the cost of operating your car to a minimum but at the same time maybe give your car some longevity. *Take the car you currently have or the used car you're thinking about buying and have it checked-out by a qualified mechanic.* Sure, we can go around the car and kick the tires, raise the hood, and drive it on the road to make sure it's OK. But is it really OK? The only way to know for sure is to have the car checked-out by a licensed mechanic. While the cost for such a service begins around $50.00 and goes up from there, it's well worth the money. Once they're done, you'll know if the car needs new brakes or ball joints or bearings. When the mechanic presents you with a written inspection you'll know if the car leaks oil or if the transmission is going out. After the mechanic has finished doing his thing, you should have a good idea if you can go on driving your car or should you begin looking for another one. If a car dealer or private owner wants to sell you a car and tells you that an inspection has been done by their garage or a friend of theirs, then go with your instincts and walk away. Better to pay the money now and have the inspection done by an impartial mechanic than to have the car break down a few minutes after you get on the freeway or a few minutes after you leave the car lot. As that old TV commercial goes, "you can pay now or you can pay later."

Read the Owner's Manual and schedule maintenance on the car according to the manufacturer's schedule. They know best! After all, this is their area. A schedule of regular maintenance (when and what) comes with all new cars. If you purchase a used car and the schedule is nowhere to be found, try going on-line or to a dealer and inquire about getting a schedule.

Use the dealer's garage for major maintenance things, but take your car elsewhere for the other items. This is definitely a "gray" area. What's major and what's not-so-major is a subjective call. If something goes wrong with a new car, I recommend taking the car to the place where you got it...especially if the car is still under warranty. Taking the car to a non-authorized mechanic may jeopardize the warranty or void it altogether. However, if your car is out of warranty or you buy a used car, find someone you trust and let them do the work as prescribed by the Owner's Manual. Performing oil changes, tune-ups, and replacing timing belts have become a regular thing for most mechanics.

> *Personally, I have my tires rotated each time I have my oil changed. It makes record keeping simple,*

Keep tires inflated and rotated. In addition to not wearing normally and increasing the chances for an accident, under or over-inflated tires can use up enormous amounts of fuel. To reduce the wear-and-tear from daily driving and to keep driving costs to a minimum, check the air pressure in your car's tires regularly. If the pressure seems low, take your car to a nearby station and get some air in the tires. The exact tire pressure that your car's manufacturer recommends is usually found in the Owner's Manual or else on the inside of the driver's side door. In addition, it is wise to rotate tires on a regular basis to ensure even wear. Personally, I have my tires rotated each time I have my oil changed. It makes record keeping simpler, saves me time, and money.

The regularity of oil changes depends on several factors including driving conditions and the weather conditions. With the increasing technology, the old adage of changing your car's oil every 3,000 miles is becoming a thing of the past. However, if you do a lot of stop-and-go driving, then 3,000 miles between oil changes may be best for you. Likewise, if you live and drive in weather conditions that are extreme, you should consider changing your car's oil on a more regular basis than a person that lives elsewhere. If you tow things like a trailer or have a high-performance engine, then 3,000 mile oil changes are something that may give extended life to your car's engine. But if you're like most drivers, then you'll be able to go longer between changes…say 5,000 to 7,500 miles. Either way, I recommend that you go by your Owner's Manual and change your oil 3 – 4 times a year but less if you drive less. If your driving requires regular oil changes, go to one of those 20-minutes or less places. You can save time and money. If you really feel adventurous, you can change the oil yourself with the only costs to you being the oil and the filter.

Regular unleaded gasoline will normally work just as well as premium gasoline in your car's tank. Again, this is not exactly my area, but I have read that all the premium, higher octane grades of gasoline does is to prevent your car from "knocking." Once again, bite the bullet, pay a little bit more at the pump, and go with what your car's manufacturer says. If push comes to shove, buy a tank or two of regular and see how your car does. Who knows, you may end-up reducing your monthly gas bill by more than you think.

Go longer between tune-ups. The traditional tune-up as we know it is slowly becoming a thing of the past. No more spending hours adjusting carburetors, setting the points, and messing with the timing. Today, most things dealing with a

> *Today, most things dealing with a car's engine are controlled by an OBC...*

car's engine are controlled by an OBC (on-board computer) and all that is left from the past is to take the old plugs out, "gap" a new set of plugs, and then put the new plugs in. This can be a big money-saver, especially if you do it yourself...like I've done! Combined, the longer times that the newer cars can go between tune-ups (as much as 50,000 to 75,000 miles) and the fact that the work can be done by a novice (like yours truly) means a person can save big bucks on car maintenance.

Doing it yourself and changing windshield wipers, air filters, and topping off brake and windshield washing fluids can also save money. I know you're going to laugh, but garages charge for things like this. Believe me, they do! The next time you get your oil changed and they present you the bill, you will see that there is a charge if they "topped-off" the fluids.   Do it yourself and save some money.

Banking

Up to about a decade ago, I admit that the whole finance and banking thing was of little, or no, interest to me. I was much more concerned about balancing my pastoral and family schedule than I was about balancing a checkbook, more committed to making withdrawals than making deposits, and more concerned with lawn-care than with ledgers. Both at church and on the home-front, I allowed others to take the lead. As a result, I quickly came to discover that I knew little about my family's money and even less about the church's money.

> *...I would like to think I have become an above-average finance person.*

Then, around the late 1990's, something happened! It was like someone flipped the "on" switch. What was once boring to me suddenly became fascinating, and what once seemed like Greek abruptly became clear and lucid. What caused that dawning of a new day is difficult to say. It may have been the fact that I was reaching middle-age, or it may have been the revelation that I was leading churches that had yearly budgets nearing the half-million dollar level. Whatever the case, a change began to take place in me. I not only became interested in finances and banking, but also I came to understand and respect the roles these two elements played in my life and, subsequently, the life of the church. Above all, I began to commit myself to learn all I could about finances and how banking works. I read, I listened, and I sought answers to questions that one would think I should (already) know.

In the years since that revelation, I would like to think I have become an above-average finance person. Yes, I know a little, but there is a great deal that I have yet to learn.

In the pages that follow, I have laid-out some things that I think will assist you as you seek not only to become a better manager of your money but also a better steward of personal finances. And who knows, maybe my suggestions will flip the "on" switch for you as you seek to reduce your banking expenses and become more intentional with the money you already have. In no particular order...

If your bank offers it, pay bills on-line. I have been doing this for nearly two years, and during that time, I calculate that I have saved between $75.00 and $100.00 yearly in postage costs alone. It's quite easy to pay bills on-line. Simply go on-line to your bank's website and follow the directions. Once set-up, you can schedule regular payments like mortgages and car insurance. In addition, you can pay those bills on-line that come in every few months or once a year like quarterly taxes and renewing your driver's license. Beyond helping me to pay on time, paying bills on-line allows me to schedule the date the bill is to be paid and then forget about them until next month. <u>Caveat</u>: be sure to record the payment in your checkbook or personal finance records. Otherwise, you're asking for big-time accounting problems.

If you can swing it, have a regular amount electronically deducted from your checking account. I have done this with my student loans and it helps tremendously. The monthly amount gets deducted at a date that I determine, and I forget about it. However, be sure to have enough in your account each month to handle the automatic debit. Forgetting will cost you dearly!

Have your employer direct deposit salary checks. In addition to not having to worry about getting to the bank to deposit your check before they close, some banks even offer free checking if a customer uses direct deposit. With more and more banks setting a limit on how many times a customer can perform teller transactions, direct deposit allows a person to save those "person-to-person transactions" for more pressing issues.

Make sure your bank is FDIC approved. Banks that are FDIC approved guarantee that accounts of $250,000 or less are covered by the government's backing. In essence, FDIC is financial insurance should something go wrong with your bank.

Use your bank's services as found on their webpage. My wife and I have four accounts at one particular bank. When we need to move money from one account to another, we simply go on-line and make the transfer without even leaving our home. Not only does this save time, but it also helps us to avoid sitting in long lines at the bank as our car continues to run and use up valuable gas.

Consider enrolling in a bank program that rounds-up the amount of your check/debit card purchases to the nearest dollar (and then puts that excess change into a savings account). The name may be different from bank to bank but the principle is the same; namely, each time you buy something with an approved card the bank will round-up that purchase to the nearest dollar amount. Then, the bank transfers that amount into a savings account. Personally, I have found this to be very helpful as I use the amount in the savings account to buy the kids their textbooks, school supplies, etc.

Keep money in interest bearing accounts as long as possible and transfer only as needed. This tact serves several purposes. First, it makes us use money more wisely because we are tricked into thinking we have less in our checking account. Secondly, it allows our money to draw interest when not being used. Lastly, keeping money in an interest-bearing account and transferring money only when needed allows money to accrue should we need it for an emergency.

When you save at the grocery store, pay your savings account. When checking-out at my local grocery store, I always ask the cashier at the store how much I saved. With this number in mind, I go home and electronically transfer that amount from my checking to my savings account. Do it quickly and it will never be missed!

Watch for free checking. Why pay money to an institution that's using your money to make money for themselves? Da!

Know the terms of your account(s). Last year, I received an unknown charge from my bank on the monthly statement. When I called they said that I had let the amount in my checking account go below a certain level. Needless to say, I pleaded ignorance. Feeling sorry for me, the branch manager had the service charge removed.

Link your savings account to the checking. Doing this will save you money and embarrassment when your account is tagged "Insufficient Funds." This way, overdrafts are "covered" by your own money and there will be no need to pay the ever-increasing fees connected with bouncing the payment.

> **Link your savings account to your checking.**

Don't be afraid to negotiate with the bank and ask them to remove the overdraft fee. Hey, we all make mistakes and think we have $1,000.00 in our checking account when we really have $100.00. Thinking it's the larger number, we then go and purchase something. Low and behold, the next day we see a charge on our checking account for insufficient funds. Many times, banks are willing to have the charge removed if we are a good customer and do not make the practice a regular one. Talk directly to the branch manager while pleading your case. It can do no damage.

Contrary to popular opinion, banks don't always have the best interest rates. As the 1960's Motown song by the Miracles says,

...Just because you've become a young man now,

There's still some things that you don't understand now.

Before you ask some girl for her hand now,

Keep your freedom for as long as you can now.'

My mama told me...'you better shop around.'

(Come on, sing it with me!)

Consider a smaller, hometown bank if you want personal service. If you want to walk into a bank where they call you by your name, then maybe a smaller bank is right for you. If you want to be able to talk to the branch manager instead of a recording, then put your money closer to home. If you want a checking account and a savings account, then look no further than down the street. However, if you want the extras a smaller bank may lack such as investment options, etc., then a bigger bank might be your best bet. Be warned: many of these services at bigger banks may not be free.

Remember that some purchases made with check/debit cards may take days to show-up on your account. Despite all the "electronic links" between stores, restaurants, and gas stations, some purchases take longer to post to our account than others. As such, we are prone to think we have more in the account than actually exists. Be careful and keep those receipts.

Coupons

Among other things, the <u>Encarta World English Dictionary</u> defines the word *coupon* this way: a voucher by a store or company that entitles somebody to a discount, refund, or gift; typically issued as a sales promotion. In general terms, I'm OK with the definition of a coupon. I'm always on the look-out for a discount, refund, or gift. However, it's the second part of the definition for coupon that gives me trouble. Particularly, the part that says "...issued as a sales promotion." Yes, as they say, that's the rub for me!

Usually, grocery manufacturers "issue" coupons because they want to push something...say, a new product. They want us to try it in hopes that we will not only buy it then but also for days, weeks, months, and years to come. Grocery manufacturers have also been known to "issue" coupons because they want to remove older items from their stock. They may have new stuff coming out, they want to completely rid themselves of a particular item, or they may feel that a certain item is not moving fast enough. Subsequently, a coupon for that item will appear in the newspaper, on-line, or in our mailbox.

Some of the coupons are good ones and really help-out with reducing grocery expenses…like the manufacturer ones that grocery stores double and even triple. Conversely, there are those coupons that draw us to items like moths to a street light…like the buy three, 32 ounce bags of shredded, sharp cheddar cheese and get 2 bags free. Granted, I like shredded, sharp cheddar cheese on nachos, tacos, and other delicacies. But what am I going to do with 10 pounds of cheese? I'm not running a food stand at a summer festival! Clearly, coupons are not always good, because they commonly cause us to buy more of something than we would normally buy or, worse yet, we end up buying items that are perishable or have a low shelf- life. Once again, we end up throwing money away.

> *…what am I going to do with 10 pounds of cheese?*

To top it off, it seems to me that manufacturers and grocery stores seem to be in cahoots! Most, if not all, coupons have an expiration date. But have you ever noticed that not long after that coupon expires that the same item goes on sale at the grocery store! Yes, the coupon for a particular washing detergent expires on October 31, but that same item will appear on sale at the same store the following week. Well, if you haven't noticed, I have.

What does all this mean? It means that there are times when we can make coupons work for us, and there are times when coupons are not-so-good. Herein lies the subject of this chapter; particularly, I want to share with you

> *...coupons are not always good,...*

some thoughts about coupons such as when to use them, when you probably need to think twice about using them, and things in-between.

Like my mother did, *make a coupon box, file your coupons in it, and be sure to note the expiration date of each coupon.* I could never figure-out my mother's system, but it worked for her! However she did it...file by product, expiration, whatever...she knew what particular item to buy and when to buy it (that is, before the coupon expired).

Watch local grocery store flyers for sales on a particular item and use the coupon then. There's nothing worse than buying an item on sale and then finding out that you had a coupon for that item. Even worse is buying an item and it's on sale the next week! The latter is out of our control, but the former is not. Pay attention, keep a list of items you need and have a coupon for, and remember to do your homework regularly of scanning grocery store ads.

Similarly, *compare shop*. Watch for those particular items in all the stores you shop by comparing specials. Then, compare prices. Finally, take your coupons to the store with the least expensive item.

Watch-out for those stores that double and triple coupons. The item(s) you purchase may cost you more even though you have a coupon.

Make a grocery list and shop each store with the intent of only purchasing items that you have a coupon for. Coupons are meant to get people into the store; because once you're in the store you're hooked. Further, retailers know that once you're in, the chances are in their favor that you'll leave with more items than you intended and spend more than you had planned.

Because you have a coupon does not necessarily mean that the item is the least expensive it can be. This is where store brands come into play. Unlike my mother, I am not a big coupon person and part of the reason may be the times. When I was growing up, my mother would shop at the grocery store closest to where we lived...mainly because we didn't have a car. Subsequently, she had to buy whatever brand the store carried and many times it was the name brand. Coupons were one of the countless ways my mother endeavored to keep food costs down.

Today, the sky is the limit, and it seems that there is a grocery store every two or three blocks. Don't you just love capitalism! More, if these grocery stores are a chain, they not only carry the big brands but also their own. Yes, right there beside the flashy-packaged, brand named potato chips are the store brand chips. Granted, you

> *Because you have a coupon does not necessarily mean that the item is the least expensive it can be.*

may have to reach up or down, but the cost of the store brand is sometimes significantly less. And if you have one of the store's customer loyalty cards, the cost between the brand name and store brand are sometimes as different as night and day.

Personally speaking, the majority of the time I prefer store brands over brand name items. For me, the taste is the same if not better, and the final reward comes when I go through the check-out line.

Bottom line: coupons are good, but seek to find-out if there is a store brand. Then, do the old taste test. If after trying the store brand you think it's not-as-good as the name brand, then watch for a manufacturer's coupon and buy the name brand. Again, do what works for you.

Debit & Credit Cards

I would be doing you and all the other readers of this work a great injustice if I did *not* say a few words about money management and personal finance especially as they relate to the use of debit and credit cards. And like so many other topics covered in this book, the opinions vary. Some favor debit cards over credit cards, and some the other way around. Personally, I tend to go in the direction of debit cards for two main reasons. First, in addition to going paperless and reducing the chance of impulse buying, my account is debited almost immediately when a purchase is made. The bill for purchases made on a credit card arrives at a later date-- as much as thirty days later. A lot could happen in those thirty days that require me to pay with cash on hand. To find out my recent purchases, I simply go on-line to my bank's website. <u>Bottom line</u>: using a debit card allows me to stay on top of my income and expenses. More, I have this fear that I will forget that I charged something and not have the funds available to pay for it. We all know what happens when credit card bills are not paid on time, right?

A second and more convincing reason why I choose to use a debit card over a credit card is that I dread the thought of owing people (in this case, the institution that issued the credit card) money. This is something that my mother felt strongly about, and I do too! Owing people and institutions money brings a great deal of unwanted things in our lives...the biggest being stress.

And yes, I am quite familiar with all the arguments on each side of the fence such as convenience, liability connected with fraud, consumer protection, and airline points. Again, this is one of those "cafeteria" things. Use what you want and leave the rest. That said, here are some things to remember about debit and credit cards.

> *Do I have enough money to pay for this item if I paid cash? If not, leave the item right where you found it.*

If you're like some people and have trouble with money management, *consider using your credit card sparingly.* Using a credit card for everyday purchases invites frivolous over-spending and even abuse. <u>A simple rule of thumb</u>: do I have the money to pay for this item if I paid cash? If not, leave the item right where you found it!

Never charge big-ticket items with a credit card. Airline tickets, major appliances, and the like...yes, but remember to pay in full and on time. Car purchases, mortgages, taxes, and the like...definitely not! God did not give us credit cards to pay for big things. Only small ones!

If you charge, *pay your bill in full as soon as it arrives.* The longer you wait to pay the bill, the greater the chance that something could happen that the credit card people will not get your payment in time. At one time or another, we have all misplaced a bill, unknowingly dropped the envelope with our payment in it in the mailbox at the local post office without a stamp, or asked someone else to mail the letter and they simply forgot to mail it. Clearly, I know of which I write! When I do

> *I know of which I write!*

charge and that is sparingly, I keep the receipt in a handy place as a reminder that I have a bill outstanding. And when the bill from the credit card people arrives, I immediately go to my on-line banking, make an EFT (electronic funds transfer), and I'm done with it. In case you've forgotten about the advantages connected with on-line banking, go back to the chapter on "B: banking" to refresh your thoughts. In addition, paying the credit card bill in full and on time saves you having to pay late charges and any possible interest.

> *...use a credit card over a debit card if that credit card gives you cash back when you do "regular" things...*

Paying only the minimum amount on a charge to a credit card will end-up costing more in the long run than the cost of the original purchase! Add to this the late fee and the possibility that the interest on the credit card will go up, all make for a lethal combination.

In addition to paying off cards with the lowest balance and those with the highest interest rate first, also consider (if possible) paying off charge cards that are nearing credit limits. Sit down with all your credit card bills and take an in-depth look at the interest rate you are being charged for credit card charges. If you owe on a charge that has an annual percentage rate of 18%, work to pay that bill off first. Then, move on to the card with the next highest interest rate and so on. As well, do all you can to pay-off those with amounts hovering around the spending limits. When a credit card is maxed-out it can affect several things including reducing your credit score and triggering additional penalties.

> *Don't fall into the trap of using any excess money...to buy other things.*

Once you have paid off one credit card, *use the money that you were paying on that card and add it to the amount you plan to pay on the next card.* Don't fall into the trap of using any excess money you may have at the end of the month to buy other things. Again, put the money that you have left-over when you finish paying a credit card bill toward any remaining credit card bills, and do it immediately. This way it won't be missed.

If push comes to shove and a recent situation has surfaced unexpectedly like a major illness or a job loss that may cause you to miss a payment or two on your credit card bill, my advice is *stop using that charge card immediately and make an instant call to the institution or bank that issued your credit card.* Remind the person on the other end of the telephone that you have always paid your charges on time; however, something has recently come-up that may cause a problem in future payments. As well, ask them for options that you may have such as reduced payments, lower interest rates, etc. The reason for doing this is clear; namely, you are showing the institution that you want to uphold your end of the deal (you purchased something and you want to pay them back). More, the institution wants their money and more times than none, they will work with you to get it. Either the institution gets their money from you at a slower rate or else they get nothing. You tell me what their decision will be?

I close with these random thoughts. First, I have not mentioned *transferring balances from one credit card to another.* In addition to calling unwanted attention on your (free) annual credit reports (see the next to last chapter entitled Y: Yahoo for free entertainment and such), it is my opinion that when we close an existing credit card account and transfer balances to a new account with a lower introductory rate we forget to ask about the rate *after* the introductory period! We may think we're getting a better rate when, in fact, the rate may be higher than the card we are currently using. In addition, *watch-out for those annual fees*. Using a card that charges an annual fee is like paying additional interest on a charge. Finally, there are definitely times when it's more financially prudent to use a credit card over a debit card. I highly suggest that you *use a credit card over a debit card if that credit card gives you cash back when you do "regular" things* like fill up your car with gas and buying groceries.

<u>Bottom line</u>: the choice of one card over another depends on the kind of card you have, how you use that card, and what card you're most comfortable using. However, you should strive to never pay interest on everyday purchases.

Education

Even as I share my thoughts with you on the ways to cut education costs, I am preparing to purchase books for my three (yes, three) kids that are currently enrolled in college. However, books aren't the only thing that will soon be "debiting" my bank account. There will be costs associated with the particular institutions they're attending, including tuition and fees, activity fees, etc. In addition, I can count on apartment rent, utilities, fees, and food. Finally, there are the transportation costs associated with them having a car such as gas and regular maintenance. As my mother used to say, "it could be worse" and she's right.

With one of the kids preparing to graduate at the end of this semester, there have been some things done that greatly reduced the "financial stress." These are categorized as before, during, and after.

Before

Get college credit while in high school. Motivated high school students can earn up to 2 years worth of college credits by taking upper level courses that offer college credit. In addition, the student may not have to pay for these classes since the cost is commonly being paid for by the high school, county, or state government. <u>A caveat</u>: make sure the student can handle these classes and also make sure these classes are transferable.

> *Complete the FAFSA as soon as the calendar year begins.*

Complete a FAFSA. Commonly called the Free Application for Student Federal Aid and based on income, this will let you know how much financial aid the student is eligible for in the coming academic year. <u>Hint</u>: complete the form not long after the new calendar year begins!

Enrolling your kids in a 529 Plan enables the residents of any state (in my case, North Carolina) to deposit funds into an interest-bearing account that will allow you to withdraw all or some of that money to pay qualified higher education expenses for an individual(s) designated as the beneficiary. Here, the beneficiaries are *my* three kids (each has an account). The state then takes my money and invests it in a plan according to my wishes (high-risk, low risk, no risk). As the "controller" of the account, I decide how much goes in and when, how much comes out and when, and where the money goes according to the plan's guidelines. When it's time to pay for one of the kid's college expenses (rent, tuition, books, etc), I simply complete a withdrawal form, send it to the agency, and they send a check out for the item.

The benefits are clear with the biggest being that a state 529 Plan is one of the few opportunities the government gives people to earn tax-free money. In my particular situation, the plan allows me to deduct the amount that I contribute into each account from my state income tax. <u>Bottom line</u>: I contribute, but I pay no state taxes on qualified college expenses.

While this may seem simple, it's a little more complex than this, so I encourage you to contact your state agency to get all the in's-and-out's of your state's plan.

Furnishings. If you know what your student may need in the way of furnishings (sheets, lamps, computers, etc), you will want to watch for sales in your local area. Start collecting now so you won't buy impulsively later. An excellent place to buy used furniture is at the local charity store (Salvation Army Thrift Store, Goodwill, etc). Why buy new, especially apartment furnishings, when the money could be better used when the student graduates and gets their first apartment.

During

Attend a community college. The average cost to attend a community college may be as much as 40% less than attending a college or university due mainly to saving money on tuition, room and board, and transportation. Once again, make sure the credits are transferable.

Do work-study. This avenue is a "win-win" for everyone including the student, parents, and institutions. For the student, they are given an opportunity to earn some money while they are taking classes. What they do with that money is their decision. They can either (a) use it as spending money (in which case the parents are not being asked every weekend to deposit more money in the student's bank account), or (b) they can apply it toward paying back their student loan. In addition, the student learns responsibility and earns valuable work experience. The parents win because it may reduce overall educational cost. Finally, the institution wins because they get work done for minimum wage!

Student loans. If not for student loans, I may not have been able to further either my undergraduate or graduate education. Student loans took up the slack when federal and state grants ended. Sadly, I am still paying even though it has been nearly fifteen years since I took out my last loan and a decade since graduating with my doctorate! While I discourage my kids from taking them out in the first place, there are some things to remember if you are considering it.

(a) Keep the amount borrowed as low as possible. The total amount and projected monthly payments may not seem that big now. However, when graduation passes and the student begins repaying the loan the amount may seem daunting since they will most likely incur other monthly expenses such rent on an apartment, car loan, and anything else associated with the move from college life to real life. My general

> *...the student should not borrow more in total than they expect or anticipate making the first year out of school.*

rule of thumb: although student lenders will gladly loan far more money than students can comfortably repay, the student should not borrow more in total than they expect or anticipate making the first year out of school.

(b) Shop around for low or no interest loans. Do all that's possible to get a federal subsidized loan such as a Perkins Loan or Stafford Loan as the government will pay any and all interest on that loan while the student is enrolled in school. Payments will begin approximately 6-months after graduation. This act alone could save hundreds, if not thousands, of dollars on the final amount to be paid on the loan. Conversely, an un-subsidized loan begins accruing interest from the day a student signs on the bottom line...and guess who pays that? Once more, do your homework here so you know how each loan works.

(c) Consider going into certain fields. The Perkins Loan could be canceled if the student works in a certain field such as public education or health care; military service, fire, or police departments; social work, public or school libraries, or non-profit organizations; or in the Peace Corps.

Books. I know this may sound extremely frugal, but when I was in graduate school my first place to check about textbooks was the library: public or university. Authors of textbooks and former students commonly donate books to libraries. So before you go buying textbooks, check out the library.

If that doesn't work, look online or on bulletin boards near where many of the student's classes will be taken. When times got rough for me, I sold my old books at cut-rate prices to buy food and pay rent and the best results came from ads I'd placed near classrooms!

As for online, it is still one of my more successful avenues when purchasing textbooks. I have discovered that the prices are less and the quality is the same. Once more, however, do your homework in finding an honest dealer.

Finally, if your state does a tax-free weekend, it is a good idea to buy textbooks and other school things then especially if the student needs a textbook or paper that is published by the college or the university. *Bottom line*: check your state's website for the date of the tax-free weekend.

After

Re-sell old textbooks. The re-selling of old textbooks is a great way to recoup *some* (I said some) of the money involved in getting a college education. Taking them to the local bookstore or exchange, selling them online, or making flyers and placing the flyers on bulletin boards near the various departments is a great way to possibly get back a return on the investment. However, this means the student must take care of the textbooks during the time they are using them.

Consolidate student loans. If a student has several student loans, it may well be worth the effort to inquire with the federal government if the loans can be consolidated into one workable loan with a lower interest rate since interest rates are now fixed. Lowering the rate over the length of the loan could save hundreds of dollars. As well, you may want to look into whether your student loan (lending) bank offers a discount if automatic payments are made.

Plead for a deal. If college loans are taking too much of a student's disposal income after graduation, they may want to ask the lender for either a graduated payment schedule (initial payments start out small and increase as income increases) or ask for an extended payment period (from 10 years to 15 or 20 years to pay back the loan).

Flying

It was not until my late teens...I was nearly 19 years old...that I first set foot on an airplane. Several weeks prior, I had hitch-hiked to Miami, Florida, to enroll in college and begin my illustrious baseball career at a small, but growing, junior college. In addition to working part-time at a convenience store across the street from my apartment, I had made the baseball team and was attending class regularly (no small feat for me at the time). Not long after receiving that first paycheck, I decided to treat myself and make a quick, weekend trip back to my hometown.

I don't remember who took me to the airport in Miami or who picked me up at the airport in Pittsburgh. As well, I don't remember how much the flight cost. However, I do remember several things about that flight even though it was over thirty-five years ago.

First, I flew on Eastern Airlines. This tells you how long ago that trip was because Eastern Airlines has been out-of-business for who knows how long. Next, I remember it was a late-night flight. As well, I remember getting food served to me. What? I don't remember! Above all, I remember sitting in an aisle seat. This proved to be a real treat because the door to the cockpit was open, and I could see out of the front of the plane. As we taxied to the runway, I could see lights as they lined the runways. And when we took that last turn and prepared for lift-off, I remember seeing a string of blue lights bordering us on both sides that seemed to lead to the horizon. Scary, isn't it? I can't remember what I had for dinner last night, but I have vivid memories of my first plane trip as if it happened yesterday. Go figure!

> *My mother could not offer any advice here because she never flew.*

It would be impossible to say how many miles I've flown since that first plane trip...clearly, it's more than a thousand but less than a million. However, what I can state with a great deal of confidence is that each time I traveled I learned more and more about how to do it for less. My mother could not offer any advice here because she never flew.

Still, does that make me an expert traveler? Definitely not. I would venture to say that my kids have flown more than me. Nevertheless, what I may lack in frequent flyer miles is made up in general, first-hand, and practical knowledge in several "flying" areas such as when to purchase the tickets in order to get the best price, when to travel, which airport to depart from, etc. Yes, in the paragraphs that follow, I offer my advice and suggestions on how you can save money flying from one place to the other. As always, my suggestions are relative and there may be some that you may not find useful. In that case, follow what I've been saying from the very beginning of this work; namely, use what you can and leave the rest for someone else.

That said, let's take-off…

If at all possible, begin your research early. The most commonly held advice is to begin researching dates, flights, and prices at least 21 days in advance but not more than six to eight weeks out. Personally, I have found that if I have a date in mind I begin 3-5 months in advance "just looking" since most airlines post their schedules anywhere from 180 days to one-year in advance. In addition, I keep a log of airlines and prices so that I know a good deal when I see one. Finally, I go into my research with a price in mind of what I can afford. <u>Bottom line</u>: it's a crap shoot! On one hand, airline fares generally begin to rise as the date of departure draws closer. Conversely, airlines need to sell seats so prices have been known to come down at the last minute. For me, if I see a fare that fits my budget on the day I'm planning to travel, I buy it and I'm done. On more than one occasion, I have played the odds...and lost.

Set-up e-mail alerts on several airlines for the route you are considering. Most, if not all, the major airlines have this service that alerts you either by computer, cell phone, or PDA, when the price to your specific destination is lowered or goes on sale. In addition, many of the "travel" websites offer the same service. The alerts are free and can save some big bucks.

Airfares can change from one hour to the next. I once read that some airlines have been known to post fare changes on their websites as many as 3 times a day through the week... mid-morning, early afternoon, and middle of the evening...depending on the time zone that the airline's headquarters are located. If it's true, then it worth the effort to pay attention if you want the cheapest airfare possible.

If possible, be flexible with dates and arriving locations. I have discovered that if a person flies on a Saturday, Tuesday, or Wednesday the fares are usually not as high as flying the other days of the week. On the other hand, I have heard others say that flying in the middle of the week (Tuesday – Thursday) brings the best fares. You say "tomato" and I say "tomatoe."

In addition, take note when fares increase and plan accordingly. If fares to Florida go up December 1, then make your reservation to fly the last of November. Planning a trip to Boston in the summer, consider flying in late August or early September when rates have been known to come down.

Likewise, do your research and see if flying to a smaller airport closer to your destination may be cheaper and more accommodating to your schedule. The savings may be well worth the little extra driving time it takes to where you want to finally end-up.

The best day and time to purchase tickets varies. I have heard it said that the best time to purchase airline tickets is late Monday or early Tuesday. Sounds reasonable, right? Most airlines change fares on Sunday nights or Monday mornings. In order to stay competitive, other airlines will follow suit in a short time. So, if a certain airline changes or lowers fares on Sunday or Monday, and the other airlines try to keep up as quickly as possible, then Monday or Tuesday is the time to compare and contrast prices!

Moreover, it may be wise to remember that most airlines change their fares on a regular basis.

If a price looks too good to be true, then you probably don't have your contacts in!

Pay attention to the "small" print. If a price looks too good to be true, then you probably don't have your contacts in! Reading the small print gives a flyer the in's-and-out's of the deal. You may have to fly the first flight out in the morning or the last flight at night. You may have to fly on certain days and to certain airports. Above all, don't make the mistake I made one time. After searching for weeks for a flight to Ft. Lauderdale, I stumbled on a fare that was going for about half of what other airlines were charging. Needless to say, I booked immediately putting in my credit card number. After hitting "submit," I was returned to the airline's homepage and a headline that read, "now choose a return flight for the same price!"

Watch for those add-ons. Upon finding a great fare, we automatically think we got the best deal when, in fact, it was far from it. By the time the taxes and fees were added, we paid for luggage, and any other fees, the cost far exceeded any competitors' fares. Again, do your homework and compare and contrast. As the old saying goes: "compare apples and apples."

Purchase on-line. The options may vary…it may be a travel website or a particular airline's website…but either way, and if it's possible, book on-line. In addition to usually getting the best fare, this will avoid you having to pay any middleman's fees.

Go on-line and review the number of sold seats. If it looks as though the flight is overbooked, plan on arriving at the airport early and getting your name on the "bumped list." If the plane is overbooked, the airline will usually ask for volunteers to take a later flight with some possible "fringe" benefits like a free ticket to anywhere the airline flies, hotel voucher, or other rewards for you giving up your seat on that particular flight. <u>Caveat</u>: be sure you know the exact terms of the deal before you go giving-up your seat.

Enroll in an airline's frequent flyer (miles) club. While I do not fly a great deal, I still have been able to fly free a few times (not including taxes, fees, etc.) as a result of me being enrolled in an airline's frequent flyer/traveler rewards program. The miles add up, and before long you've earned a freebie. However, I caution you on two fronts. *One*: do not pay one penny to be a member of the airline's frequent flyer club. *Second*: do all you can to know the terms of the membership. Some airlines have a policy whereby miles have to be redeemed within a certain amount of time. In other words, "use them or lose them."

If your budget allows it, pay for your tickets using a credit card that gives you air miles. If you have such a card, then use it wisely (i.e. paying on time). Otherwise, you may end-up paying for the cost of the airline ticket several times over...you know what I mean! If you do not have a particular airline's credit card and are thinking about it, then do all you can to become familiar with the terms of the card such as annual fee, blackout travel dates, etc.

Will a package deal work? If you are planning to make a trip and will need a rental car and a hotel, see what kind of a deal you can get if you "lump" all three (air fare, hotel room, and car rental fee) into one. Nearly all of the major travel websites allow you to do such a comparison. To make sure it's really a deal, compare each of the elements separately.

...see what kind of a deal you can get if you "lump" all three (air fare, hotel room, and car rental fee) into one.

You may have noticed that I have stayed away from the other areas related to flying like how and what to pack, how to get through security lines faster, the best airports for airport food, etc. I've done this on purpose; namely, because these elements vary from person-to-person and deal mainly with the issue of time and not money!

Groceries

Later on in this work, I share with you some common marketing techniques that stores employ to "encourage" us to buy things. Among these techniques are intentionally designing and building stores with narrow aisles, placing the most expensive and brightly-decorated items at eye level, and placing non-sale items along-side sale items. The particular chapter is entitled "W: Watch-out for these store tricks."

In this chapter, though, I want to share with you some cost-savings ways to save you money at the local grocery store where you shop. This is one of those "smaller" chapters that I wrote about in the introduction, so it will not be as long as some of the other chapters in this work. As always, some of these methods you may already know and employ. Hopefully, what I offer will only add to your money-managing skills.

Plan your weekday meals. Few things can increase the monthly grocery bill more than buying food items on an "as needed" basis. You're all ready to serve spaghetti tonight for dinner, but at the last minute you remember that you're out of pasta. So, you jump in the car, fight traffic, and slow check-out lines to get that one box of noodles. As you stand in line, you notice the person on the adjacent check-out line has a container of parmesan cheese. Immediately, you jump out of line and begin making your way to aisle 5...international foods. When you return to check-out you discover that half the people in your city are in line to check-out and each of them has a shopping cart overflowing with food! If you would have only planned ahead, you would have not only been able to spend less money but also may have been able to control your level of frustration, especially in light of the fact that when you got home you discovered that your family had gone ahead and ordered Chinese food to be delivered!

Bottom line: in planning meals, we make fewer trips to the grocery store thus spending less money. More, making less often trips to the grocery store cuts down on impulsive buying.

Make a list. This will help reduce the chances of you buying on impulse. In addition to providing you some direction for what grocery things you'll need for the week, a list will also help you stay focused on need and not wants.

Check out the store flyer. After you get your grocery cart, look just inside the store doors and chances are real good that you'll see the store flyer. There, you have the store's specials for that week. Take a minute or two, go over the ads with a fine tooth comb, and see what you need. Better yet, go on-line and check-out all the neighboring store's specials and compare prices.

<u>Caveat</u>: commonly, grocery store specials run from mid-week to mid-week (i.e. begin on Wednesday and run through Tuesday). In addition to familiarizing yourself with your store's schedule, be sure to do your homework and see about neighboring stores.

Clip coupons. I've already covered this in an earlier chapter (C: coupons), so let's move on to other money-savings things. Nevertheless, several things in parting. First, don't purchase a food item just because you have a coupon. Next, watch for which stores double and triple coupons and when they do it. In addition, buy only what you need with a coupon. Finally, watch for those BOGO items especially when you have a coupon.

Don't go hungry or with the kids. Nothing increases grocery costs like going to the store hungry. Everything looks good. Am I right? When we go to the grocery store hungry we come home with things that we would probably not buy otherwise like pork rinds, French onion dip, and a loaf of bread that's round and unsliced instead of long and rectangular. As well, don't go to the store with kids (if you can help it). With three kids, every time they went with me to the grocery store it always cost me more! It's like that book about the Berenstain Bears on the gimme's. No parent knows more pressure than standing in a check-out line with kids screaming and crying because we didn't get the cereal with a Transformer inside or the one with an American Girl on the front of the box.

> ### Don't go hungry or with the kids.

Ask yourself if you can save money buying in bulk. If so, save yourself time and money by becoming a member of the local food warehouse. Then, buy the 5 pounds of pasta, divide the bag into five smaller bags, and use as needed. As for meat and similar items, it's the same principle...divide and conquer. <u>Caveat</u>: unless I'm planning to use them quickly, I avoid buying perishables like fruits and vegetables at food warehouses because of the item's limited shelf life. If I do buy these items in bulk, I try using them as added ingredients to dishes that can be frozen or will keep for several days.

Buy generic. They commonly cost less and the taste is equal to name brands. Try them out, and if you think otherwise, you can always go back.

Don't forget outlet stores. Cookies seem to go fast in this house, and since they do, why pay full price for something that turns-over quickly. A favorite place for cookies for me is the local Pepperidge Farms outlet. The same holds true for bread. I know of more and more cities that have a bread outlet that sells bread and bakery items that are time sensitive for less.

Pay attention to the unit price. This will tell you how much an item costs per ounce, pound, etc. In like fashion, the unit price allows you to compare prices of that item with other similar items.

Familiarize yourself with an item's price and make sure that price rings-up when you check-out. Mistakes happen all the time at grocery stores and some go unnoticed by both customers and cashiers. To avoid paying more for an item than it was marked on the shelf, make sure to watch the price when it's scanned. Don't be afraid to challenge the price. Who knows maybe it was a computer error or the price was programmed wrong into the computer.

> *Who knows maybe it was a computer error or the price was programmed in wrong...*

Get a grocery store frequent shopper card. Depending on the store, these cards come in many names including Plus, VIC, and MVP. Still, the principle remains; namely, the item will cost less if you have one of these cards.

Health & Gym Fees

I am proud to say that I have never, never had membership in one of those big name gym or health clubs. One needs only to put me on the scales for proof! In addition to the length of the contracts which can go as long as two years or more, it seems that health and fitness clubs are open one day and closed the next! And when a club does go out of business and closes, what do you think opens up in that same building...you guessed it, another health club.

Still, there are some ways to save money on health and gym membership fees. But before we tackle the issue, you need to ask yourself some questions...

Will I really use a gym or health club? Currently, my wife and I have membership in the local (city) recreation center. It's not a big center, mind you, but it has what we want, need, and use. It has a small exercise area with free-weights, treadmills, and an exercise bike. In addition, the 25-meter swimming pool is great for lap swimming and the changing room has showers and lockers. That's it! There is no juice bar or racquetball courts. Clearly, this gym has everything we need (well, truth is, we could use another treadmill). My wife and I work-out to stay in-shape and *not* to train for the Olympics. More, the hours of operation fits our schedule. Best of all is the price...less than $500.00/year for the both of us.

Bottom line: when you look at a gym or health club, ask yourself what exercise equipment will you really need and will you use that membership to the fullest.

How far is it from my home or place of business? I figure the further away a gym or health club is from home or business the less I will use it. If it's close or you pass by it on the way home, then it may be just what you're looking for in the realm of convenience. In addition, I have found that if a gym or health club is on the way home I am "guilted" into using it (you know, passing by each day and not stopping I feel that I am wasting my money).

Finally, you need to ask *if you can afford the monthly or yearly membership.* At our recreation center, you can take out membership on a monthly, quarterly, or yearly basis. We take out membership quarterly because we can exercise outside during most of the year.

Now that you've decided that yes, you do want to take out membership in a health club or gym, and that you will use the membership because it's close to your home or business and it fits your finances, then it's time to explore the ways you can save money on a membership but still get all the benefits.

Look at your contract carefully. Pay strict attention to such areas as renewal contract (does it automatically renew or do you have to renew periodically), cancellation clauses (what if you move), any penalties for late payments, and what if the place is closed for repairs or you get hurt (is the contract extended or is it a "use or lose" deal). As well, be sure that it states in your contract the in's-and-out's of transferring to other gyms, allows guests, and what specifically your contract includes (i.e. exercise room but not pool, extra classes, etc). Finally, be sure to ask if there is a "release clause" if you're not happy and what happens if the gym is sold to another owner.

> *Don't be shy. Ask if there are any discounts for age,...*

Ask about any discounts. Don't be shy! Ask if there are discounts for age, place of employment, or clubs or organizations that you belong to. Ask if you get a discount if you pay in full or have the monthly fee debited from your bank account.

Is there a gym where you work? If so, jump on the exercise wagon and get going. Be sure to tell your employer that you are exercising and maybe you'll get a reduction in your health premiums. If not, does your employer have some kind of deal with a nearby health club or gym?

Is there a college or university nearby? Some college and universities offer gym memberships to alums. If not, does a nearby hotel have any kind of gym membership with its facilities?

Work-out at home or in a nearby park. A cemetery is a great place to walk since there's not a lot of chitter-chatter, loud music, or grunting going on as you exercise.

Bottom line: follow my lead on this one and ask yourself 5 things...

- Am I really going to use the membership?
- Is it close to home or business?
- Do the gym hours fit my hours?

- Does it have the amenities that I want?
- Can I afford it?

If you answer *"yes"* to all of these, then I suggest you go for it!

Insurance: Car, Health, and Home

If there is one item that puts nearly all Americans in the same boat, it has to be that we all have, and pay for, some kind of insurance. Yes, nearly all of us pay a premium for either car, health, or homeowner's insurance. And when we have all of these as I do, the combined amount in premiums can be staggering. I know this as a fact, because each month these three alone (my car insurance, my health insurance, and my homeowners insurance) takes-up...on average...nearly 10% of my monthly income before taxes. A "short list" of my insurance coverage includes monthly (a) car insurance on three cars with coverage on my wife, one of the kids, and me; (b) health insurance; and (c) homeowner's insurance. In addition, I pay a monthly premium for life insurance and yearly premiums for wind and hail coverage (since we live near the North Carolina coast) and flood insurance because our house in Washington is located near the flood plain. Again, I figure that nearly 10% of my monthly income involves paying insurance premiums alone!

However disheartening this may sound, my overall premiums may be a great deal lower than the premiums of others because of several factors including higher deductibles, select coverage, and driving record. And how did I get a financial handle on insurance premiums...I did my homework. I read, I researched, and I reviewed what I needed in the way of coverage and what I could afford. Simply put: I familiarized myself with the "lay of the land," and the savings started immediately thereafter.

In the lines that follow, I want to share with you some, if not all, of the things I did to lower my insurance premiums but still retain adequate coverage for everyone

> *Safety and providing for the future needs of others... should never be compromised in order to save a few dollars.*

involved. Once more, this is not a complete list by any means, but it is a beginning. More, it is a proven list that worked for me and will hopefully work for you. Still, I caution you that insurance is a very serious area and must not be entered into lightly. Safety and providing for the future needs of others are two areas that never should be compromised in order to save a few dollars. When in doubt, see an expert in the field.

Since buying insurance takes time and education, let's start by looking not only at what most insurance policies have in common but also what separates them from each other. Following, I want to breakdown each category (car, health, and homeowners) with an eye toward how I reduced my insurance premiums.

Similarities

Adjustments may occur in monthly premiums depending on certain factors. Age, record, and number of claims may all play a factor in determining monthly premiums.

Benefits. All polices have some kind of explanation of what is and is not covered by the policy.

Coverage. All insurance policies have an area of coverage that guarantees the holder is and will be protected should an accident occur with a legitimate claim.

Deductibles. As explained briefly in the next chapter (J: jargon), a deductible is a portion of a claim that must be paid prior to the insurance carrier paying their part. Normally, it is a fixed, agreed upon amount, and the higher the deductible means the lower the premiums. With the exception of life insurance policies, nearly all insurances have a deductible. The range of deductibles varies from $250.00 to as much as $5,000.00.

Termination of coverage. Should premium payments cease, shortly thereafter, the insured losses their coverage.

Differences

Renewal. Some insurance policies require semi-annual renewal (every 6 months) such as car insurance, while other polices are renewed annually (health and homeowners insurance).

Some policies have preventive elements. Health insurance policies commonly allow the insured to have one or more preventative elements to be performed such as yearly physicals and eye exams. While there are things that individuals can do to reduce their insurance rates such as enrolling in defensive driving classes or protecting their homes by installing smoke or burglar alarms, these are not what I would call preventative acts.

Limits. Some policies put a limit on how much

the insurer will cover should a claim be filed.

Lifestyles and habits. Whereas a smoker or an inexperienced driver may affect health or car insurance premiums, the same could not be said about the premiums regarding homeowners insurance.

With the similarities and differences between car, health, and homeowner's insurance now behind us, let's quickly move on to the ways that you can not only become a better money manager but also a better steward of the money you have. Let's begin with car insurance...

Car Insurance

Avoid monthly installment charges by paying premiums in full each year. Most insurance companies give their customers an option to pay monthly, quarterly, every six-months, or once a year. Keep in mind that the more often you pay the more administrative charges are connected to that policy. To reduce your costs, try to pay once a year. If not, then every six months. A simple installment charge of $3.00 tacked-on to your monthly car insurance bill adds $36.00 to the bottom line of your premiums.

Keep track of your credit scores. Your credit score (that is, your history of paying bills on time) plays a factor in determining your car insurance premiums. Since a clean slate means a reduced rate, go on-line and order a free credit report (see the chapter titled Y: Yahoo for free entertainment and such).

Try to drive less and park your car off the street. Insurers commonly ask their clients how often and how far they drive to-and-from work. The reason: the more often we drive and the farther we drive the greater the chance we will become involved in an auto accident (the odds are against us). One way to reduce car insurance premiums is to drive less (consider car

> *Try to drive less and park your car off the street.*

pooling or taking mass transit to work).

Likewise, avoid parking your car on the street at night because increased traffic also increases the chances of someone running into it.

If your car is over ten years old, consider dropping the collision coverage. As defined in the next chapter, collision insurance is the coverage that pays to repair the driver's car if the driver is at fault. <u>A question to ask</u>: is the cost I'm paying for collision coverage more than the "fair market value" of the car? If it is, drop the collision insurance.

Compare rates and coverage. Go on-line and compare rates of several companies. To avoid any confusion and to compare apples to apples, make a chart and include the company, the deductible, the amount of coverage, etc. Rely more on written facts than memory!

Ask about any and all discounts. Ask if the company gives discounts for good driving records, good grades by your young drivers, defensive driving classes, or any professional groups, alumni associations, or organizations that you are involved in. If the carrier does mention discounts, you ask them! *BTW* (aka: by the way): (1) Ask at what future date will the rates for your young driver go down? Usually after a young driver has been driving for 3 years or so and has a clean driving record, the rates will come down for them. (2) If your young driver has a car at college, make sure the insurance carrier knows it. In addition to being truthful, the rate may come down especially if they are attending a college in a small town.

Do you really know what you have and do you need all of those coverages? Granted, we have all the biggies on our car insurance policy, including medical, liability, uninsured/underinsured, etc, but do we really need to have some of the other "coverages" like towing and rental cars. Simply put: know what you have and ask if something can go. We pay a yearly fee to AAA and that covers towing should one of the cars breakdown.

> *Remind your drivers that good reports (and grades) means lower rates.*

Look at your insurance needs every 6 months. Things change and so do circumstances. Soon after one of the kids had been driving for 3 years with a spotless record, I went back and started getting new quotes for car insurance. You can image my surprise when the rates for him went down nearly 50%!

Remind your drivers that good reports (and grades) means lower rates. From speeding tickets to fender benders, nearly everything can negatively affect insurance rates. As well, remind them that good driving records pays off in lower rates.

Don't let your coverage lapse. If you allow your car insurance to lapse...even a week or so...it will cost you. Most states charge a fine to the policy's owner for such a no-no. If anything, ask your (new) carrier if they will take care of changing over the policy for you.

If you switch carriers in the middle of a year and you've paid for the year, make sure your "old" carrier gives you a refund. The top of your insurance policy lists the dates that the policy covers (usually six months). I try to terminate one coverage and begin another as close to the ending dates as possible. That way, I don't have to worry about refunds or being short-changed.

Raise your deductible. Increasing your deductible from $250.00 to $1,000.00 may reduce your premiums dramatically over the course of a year. Granted, you will pay more up-front when an accident occurs, but do as I do...raise the deductible and put the money you save in an interest bearing account. Then, when an accident occurs (and it will, believe me), you will not only have the money to pay the deductible but you may have also earned some interest from your money.

Lump policies. Some insurance companies will reduce the cost of premiums if the owner has more than one policy (auto and homeowners) with the carrier. Conversely, do your homework to see if separate policies for auto and homeowners may be cheaper.

Health Insurance

Evaluate your medical needs yearly. Like car insurance, your health insurance options need to be reviewed annually. Have you gotten married in the past year? Did a son or daughter graduate from college and are now on their own? Would it be cheaper for you to go on your spouse's or partner's plan or vice-versa?

Know the in's-and-out's of your plan. A sudden trip to the ER on January 1st is no time to learn that the limits of your plan changed on December 31. The details of the plan may be confusing, so take your time reading it. If you're still confused, ask a person with some knowledge in the area to give you a synopsis of the plan.

Consider setting-up a HSA (health savings account). This practice allows a person to deposit pre-tax dollars into an account and use these funds to pay for medical needs such as out-of-pocket expenses, co-pays, and deductibles.

Go to an Urgent Care place instead of the ER. For more detail about this element, go to the chapter titled "M: miscellaneous."

Ask the doctor for samples or to prescribe a generic brand of medicine. Many times, doctors will get free samples of new drugs by drug manufacturers. Simply ask your doctor if they have any that fits your particular situation. If not, then ask if the prescription comes in a generic brand.

Homeowner's Insurance

Ask your carrier for advice. Many times, homeowner's insurance can be reduced somewhat by doing some simple things around the house things like installing smoke alarms, dead bolts on exterior doors, purchasing fire extinguishers, motion-sensitive lights, etc.. For a complete list, ask your insurance carrier.

Raise your deductible. As stated earlier, put what you save by raising your deductible into an interest-bearing account

Don't add the value of the land when getting a quote.

and then use the savings to not only pay your deductible but also earn some interest.

Don't add the value of the land when getting a quote. A common mistake when people go to get homeowner's insurance is that they will look at the value of their place according to local tax assessments. Wrong! You're wanting to insure the house and its contents and not the land.

Shop around. This is America and we are a capitalist country. It's everybody for themselves so share the wealth.

Pay yearly instead of monthly. Again, this saves on monthly fees and charges.

Use all your discounts. Ask your carrier if you can get a discount because of where you live (within 100 feet of a hydrant and less than 1 mile from a fire station), what organizations you belong to (AARP, alumni,

> *Pay yearly instead of monthly.*

professional organization, etc), and what kind of rates are possible if you put your auto and home on the same policy.

Document. While you will never get paid in full what you lose (be it physical or emotional), you need to do all you can to get things as close to what they were as before. And while you're evaluating insurance needs, consider taking a yearly inventory of your possessions by writing down what you have, when you purchased it, and what it cost you when purchased. Better yet, you may want to have someone do a video tape of the contents your home.

Know your policy. As with auto and health insurance, not knowing what your policy covers and does not cover will hurt you...physically, financially, and definitely, emotionally!

Jargon:
terms to be familiar with

As an avid sports person, I know a little about all sports and a great deal about baseball. For example, I know how to determine a pitcher's ERA (Earned Run Average), a batter's OBP (On-Base Percentage) and his OSP (On-base Slugging Percentage). Conversely, ask me about the term Ashes, ferret, and Out-dipper as they relate to the game of Cricket, and I'm lost. If I knew the terms and what they meant, it would help me to understand the game, right?

Such is the case with many of the terms that I use in this book. If you knew what the term meant, things might be clearer to you when they are used.

In this section of the work, I have taken several of the terms that I have used or will use in the book and defined them for you. In every sense of the word that defines this chapter, here are some words, jargon, if you will, that you need to be familiar with if you are to become a better money manager and steward of your personal finances. Again, this is just a few of the words you need to know.

BOGO –
Buy one of something and get one thing of the same item for free.

Brothers (and sisters) –
My siblings in descending order according to age: Cheryl, Frank, Rodney, Melissia, and David. I "fit" between Rodney and Melissia.

Caveat (emptor) –
A Latin phrase that means "let the buyer beware." If there's something wrong with the stuff, too bad! You can't go after the guy for selling you a lemon. In other words, look out!

Collision insurance –
For automobiles, this type of insurance covers damage to a car if the driver is at fault. Since this coverage usually pays for repairs up to the "fair market value" of the car, most owners drop this coverage after the car reaches ten years or older.

Comprehensive insurance –

For automobiles, this type of insurance pays to repair or replace the owner's car and anything inside the car if the loss is related to fire, theft, or vandalism.

Credit card –

With a credit card, the issuer, usually a bank or lending institution, allows a person to purchase goods or services and pay for them later (usually with interest).

Debit card –

With a debit card, the funds used to pay for a specific purchase are withdrawn directly (and usually immediately) from the bank account once the card is used.

Deductible –

The portion of a claim that is normally fixed and must be paid prior to the insurance carrier paying their part.

DNR –

Do Not Resuscitate. In medical situations, a DNR is an instruction or command from a person that they or a loved one are not to be resuscitated if that person should suffer from cardiac or respiratory arrest.

EFT –
Also known as Electronic Funds Transfer, many banks have a service that allows customers to pay bills electronically. This service can save hundreds of dollars in postage.

FDIC –
Better known as the Federal Deposit Insurance Corporation, the actions are exactly as the title implies. The federal government guarantees the safety of deposits up to $250,000 per person per bank among its member banks.

Frequent flyer miles –
Airline travelers enrolled in such a program can accumulate points (miles) for each mile they fly with a certain carrier. They can then redeem the miles for free airline travel in the future or receive an upgrade. Some credit card companies offer miles when the customer charges items on the card.

HDL –
Known as high-density lipoprotein or good/happy protein, HDL is related to the cholesterol levels in your blood. The ideal level for HDL is between 40 – 60.

ICE –

"In case of emergency." Put this in your cell phone list of frequently called numbers. In case of an emergency, this will tell EMT's, police, and fire responders who they should call should you be involved in an accident.

Kids –

I have three: Zachary (the oldest), Joshua (the purest definition of a middle-child), and Hannah Rose (the youngest). They are also known as: the three stooges; those three wharf-rats; and Discount, Net, and Reduced (Price, get it!)

Liability Insurance –

For automobiles, this type of insurance covers other people's bodily injuries or death that may result from your fault. This kind of auto insurance also covers you if someone tries to bring legal action against you for damages you may have caused.

LDL –

Known as low-density lipoprotein or bad/lousy protein, LDL is related to the cholesterol levels in your blood. The ideal level for LDL is less than 100.

Mt. Rainier cherries –
Quite possibility, the best fruit on the face of this earth.

New Martinsville -
Located five miles south of the Mason-Dixon Line in the northern panhandle of West Virginia, the city of approximately 5,600 residents and lies along the banks of the Ohio River.

Powerball –
A multi-state lottery game in which players pick 5 numbers and a Powerball for a chance to win millions, tickets cost $1 each, and my path on which to become a millionaire!

Public assistance -
Also known as welfare, these government-based programs help low-income families with assistance in the form of food stamps, medical care, etc.

Vehicles –
For the record, I drive a 1998 Volvo (my fourth) and it currently has 125,000 miles on it (my last one, a 1987 Volvo, had 268,000 miles on it before I sold it to the local junk yard for $200.00). My wife drives

a 1999 Acura, and just the other day the odometer turned 198,000 miles.

West Virginia –
As the late John Denver aptly put it: "Almost Heaven." Need I say more? Became the 35th state of the union on June 20, 1863, when Virginia seceded.

Work-study –
Designed for college students, it is a government-based program that provides part-time employment to help off-set the cost of college.

Kids

With all three kids now in college and pretty much on their own, they've arrived at the stark reality that if they want something or want to do something outside the bounds of "normal parental financial support"...they have to pay for it themselves. Yes, the college thing and most everything connected with it including apartment rent, food, tuition, and books are paid for them (at least until they've completed 8 semesters...after that, they're definitely on their own). As well, the car things are taken care of including insurance, regular maintenance, and new parts. As for everything else they may feel they're entitled to, they must pay for themselves, including leisurely getaways to the beach, laundry, and a regular supply of libations.

As a result, they seem to have had a revelation. The revelation is that things cost money! Clearly, all that they've been told over the years about money matters has finally sunk in. It's like the quote from humorist Mark Twain when he said, "When I was a boy of 14, my father was so ignorant I could hardly stand to have the old man around. But when I got to be 21, I was astonished at how much the old man had learned in seven years."

And with that, some advice...financial and otherwise... that I have learned as it relates to kids.

Don't let your kids lend-out the car to their friends. Although the friend's insurance may cover an accident even when they drive your kid's car, the policy owner that the car is registered to/with may have some liability and be on-the-hook for any further financial awards.

> *Don't let your kids lend out the car to their friends.*

Discourage your kids from lending their friends money. It's one thing to lend money...we sometimes never get it back. Even worse, though, is having to ask for that money back and the hard feelings that go along with such a "transaction."

Encourage your kids to talk over how bills, food,

etc., will be paid if they have roommates. Few things create such ill-feelings (emotional and financial) among roommates more than failing to discuss and not arriving at a clear understanding of the division of bills, when they are to be paid, etc. From experience, I have learned that all the names of the roommates should be on the lease and on all utility bills. In addition, hold firm and say "no" if your student wants a landline in the apartment.

Warn them about using ATM's that are out of their bank's system. At $3.00 - $5.00 a transaction, using ATM's outside one 's banking system can add-up quickly.

No matter the incentives, discourage your student from taking out a credit card on campus. The combination of over-extending their income, not paying on time, and late fees is a usually a recipe for short and long-term financial disaster. If they insist on a credit card, (a) let them get the card in their name but you (the parent/parents) co-sign, and (b) remind them of the importance of paying the bill on time and how doing so relates to the future (i.e. good credit scores, etc).

Have the utility company send the bills electronically to all the roommates. More is less, and considering the amount of time students spend on-line, the chances of the bill getting "lost" or "misplaced" is reduced.

If possible, do not allow your student to have a car on campus the first semester. There are several benefits to doing this, including lower fuel bills, the student will feel less tempted to go out when they should be studying thus (possibly) spending less money, and your auto insurance rates could go down (at least temporarily). However, make sure the student knows that they can't get behind the wheel of anyone else's car unless insurance is somehow provided for them. Bottom line: if they're not driving one of the family cars, it may be best to tell them they shouldn't be driving at all.

> **Do not allow your student to have a car on campus the first semester.**

Carefully examine their on-campus food plan. Commonly, students can chose from a variety of food plans ranging from 21 meals a week to 10 or 12. Consider starting at the lower end. If they need more, you can always add to the plan. Keep in mind that it doesn't work the other way...if they have a 21 meal plan and use only 14 meals, the rest is forfeited. As for off-campus, do as I do and give them a set amount of "food money" each week. <u>Caveat</u>: you may want to go to the grocery store with them. This way you can see if they are spending the money correctly and buying wholesome and nutritious foods and not "drinking their meals!"

Let the student see the bill from the college or university. I would bet that most students, mine especially, have no idea the cost of higher education. As I have done before, let them see the itemized bill that lists tuition, fees, housing, etc. And why you're at it, check and see if your student is being charged to use the health center or for health insurance. If so, contact the school and get them removed from the bill. Why pay twice, especially if what the school offers duplicates what you already have!

Remind your student to always (and I mean always) ask for student discounts when they go out. One just never knows when a restaurant, movie place, theater, etc, will offer a student discount.

Tell them to take care of their textbooks, especially if they're planning to sell them at the end of the semester. Textbooks that bring the highest re-sale price are those books that are sparingly highlighted, the covers are in good shape, and no pages are missing. Moderate care today means higher prices tomorrow!

Remind them the importance of taking care of vital documents. In other words, they need to do all they can to protect their Social Security card, ATM card, credit cards, driver's license, and checkbook. One needs only to say to them the words: identity theft.

Make a written contract with them that if they get a ticket or are involved in an auto accident, they pay for any increases in the car insurance premiums. I have found this approach acts as a great deterrent!

Would it be better if they had a debit card instead of a credit card? I have discovered that with a debit card the chance of racking-up high credit card charges is reduced greatly. Beyond being able to electronically "track" most purchases, a debit card can be linked to a savings account. If the student goes over the amount in their account, the amount of the purchase will be automatically debited from the savings account. In turn, this may save from having to pay for overdraft fees and bank charges.

Buy used furniture. I (absolutely) refuse to buy

> ## *I (absolutely) refuse to buy new furniture for my kid's apartments.*

new furniture for my kids' apartments. With the amount of traffic and daily wear-and-tear that happens in the course of an academic year, the question of whether to buy new furniture is a "no brainer." Good quality and great deals can be found at second-hand stores. Hold-off buying the new stuff until after they graduate.

Legal Stuff

I'm embarrassed to admit it, but I did *not* compose anything connected to my (future) death including a will, living will, or designate a power of attorney for health care until last summer! I know that sounds strange, but it's true...and the only reason I did it then was because my wife and I were going out of the country. All this got me to thinking about what happens after I'm gone or who will make medical decisions if I'm not able. With that, a few thoughts on how to make things easier (financially, physically, and emotionally) for those around me.

Do a will. Two of the prime reasons a person chooses to compose a will is (a) to reduce any possible conflict over money or property and (b) to avoid the state from intervening and deciding how to split-up the assets of the estate. With that, a person should review periodically their assets, including property, life insurance policies, and all bank accounts. From there, the person should decide who should be included in the will and what portion of the estate each person listed in the will should receive.

Do a living will. This will tell doctors exactly what kind of care you desire should you become terminally ill or incapacitated and not able to make decisions yourself. While lawyers can draw one of these up for you, a more inexpensive way is to go to the local hospital and ask for one. Although most hospitals require a person to attend a seminar, the details covered in such a seminar are invaluable. Above all, a living will removes loved ones from having to make difficult decisions such as the use of feeding tubes, how long to stay on a ventilator, and whether or not to resuscitate (DNR). Blank templates can also be found online. Whatever the course one chooses, the decision must be well thought-out, witnessed and signed by three people, and documented.

Power of attorney. Briefly, the power of attorney acts as proxy spokesperson in financial and medical matters. The power of attorney should be a person that is knowledgeable, honest, and trusted. After all, they will be the ones speaking on your behalf.

Miscellaneous

If your house is anything like my house, then you undoubtedly have a "junk drawer." You're smiling because you not only know what I'm talking about but you also have one. Wherever it's located...either in the kitchen or in the den...the "junk drawer" is that one drawer in your house that has all kinds of stuff in it. The stuff may not seem that important, but on the other hand you don't want to throw anything away because the minute you do you'll end-up needing it the next day! Take keys, for example. I must have a hundred of them in my "junk drawer" in Washington. God only knows what they fit. Still, you can bet that as soon as I throw one of them in the trash, the next day I'll find something locked that needs a key to it get unlocked.

This chapter and "junk drawers" are a lot alike. For several reasons, I have appropriately titled this chapter *Miscellaneous*. First, this chapter has a lot of things in it that are useful tools for me in helping you to become a better steward and money manager. For some reason, I just couldn't find a place for them in another chapter. Rather than discard them, I have put them in this chapter. Next, I wanted to share them with you because you just never know when you'll need them. To exclude them is to be very subjective. In addition, I put them in this chapter because they are important tools for personal finance and I did not want them to get lost among other things in some other chapter. These are not just random thoughts. These are things that I have seen my mother do, things I have heard and seen church members do, and things that I have done to make ends meet. Finally, for simplicity and organization, I've put these money-wise, cost-saving, and expense-reducing tips in alphabetical order. Remember, the sub-title of this work is *The A, B, C's of Pinching Pennies like a Pastor*.

> **Remember, the sub-title of this work is The A,B,C,'s of Pinching Pennies like a Pastor.**

As always, pick the ones you want and are beneficial to your particular circumstances and leave the rest in the "junk drawer."

Avoid using money machines that are outside your bank's network. If you have withdrawn money recently from an outside ATM, did you note how much you're being charged? The institution that issues the money charges a fee and your bank charges a fee. More, these fees range from a few dollars to quite a few dollars. The solution is to note the locations where your banking institution have their machines and use them. If you are traveling, go on-line and do the same.

Begin keeping a loose change jar. This needs little, if any, explanation. You simply put all loose change you have at the end of a day in a big jar. I use the change for vacation money. For a different kind of slant, I also use that jar for laundry money...no, not what you think! At one point, I did not have a washer and dryer. As such, I had to go to the local laundry-mat and spend $5.00 - $10.00 each time to get my laundry done. A few years ago someone in church gave me a small washer and dryer. Now, each time I wash my clothes, I put the money that I would have used at the laundry-mat in the change jar.

Choose Primary or Urgent Care places over going to the Emergency Room whenever possible. In addition to seeing you sooner, choosing a Primary or Urgent Care place (I call them "doc in the box") over going to an Emergency Room will save you money. At an ER, you most likely will end-up paying an attending doctor and the hospital for the visit after your insurance has paid its share. Whereas, a Primary or Urgent Care visit will commonly be paid by your insurance.

Don't you dare purchase reading glasses at some eye care center! Come on, they're reading glasses. Purchase a designer pair of everyday reading glasses at your optometrist or eye care center and you could pay upwards of $100.00. Instead, I suggest you go to a discount place and buy the same pair of glasses minus the flashy frames for one-tenth of that price. My last pair of reading glasses I bought at Ace Hardware for $4.95.

> *My last pair of reading glasses I bought for $4.95 at Ace Hardware.*

Evaluate your entertainment choices periodically. Do you really need to have 100+ cable channels? Do you really need to have HBO, Showtime, and all those other pay-per-view stations? You can only watch one at a time, right? Cable packages are usually tiered, so choose one that fits your particular situation. And while you're at it, you do not need to be renting $5.00+ movies. Go to one of those red kiosks and get a movie for $1.00.

Furnace and air-conditioning filters need to be changed regularly, so don't forget. Since the frequency that filters need to be changed depends on how much the unit is used, I have found it useful to write the date the filter is installed/changed on the outside of the filter. While most of the newer programmable units have a reminder, I try to change my filters every 2 or 3 months. A clogged or dirty filter makes the unit run more thus using extra energy.

> *A clogged or dirty air filter makes the unit run more thus using extra energy.*

Generic brands of food commonly cost less but still offer high taste and good quality. <u>My simple rule of thumb</u>: if I'm going to use a food item with something else, generic will do. Why use a name brand mayonnaise that costs so much more than the generic when you'll be mixing that mayonnaise with tuna to make tuna salad?

Hang-out your laundry, if possible. Have you ever started your dryer and then gone outside to look at your electric meter? If you have, then surely you have noticed that once that 220-volt dryer gets going the little dial on the electric meter begins spinning faster than a kitchen blender! Personally, I love the fresh smell of drying-off with a towel that's been hung-out on the clothes line.

Install timers or motion sensors on outside lights. Nothing bugs me more than getting up in the morning, going outside, and finding that I'd left a light on all night. Once again, I'm throwing money away.

Join with friends in the neighborhood, at work, or from church and start a walking club. Nothing demands more from us than knowing that we've made a commitment and people are counting on us. Once the club is started, you can then cancel that gym or health club membership once your membership expires.

Keep a file of when you'll be eligible for Social Security and how much you will get upon retirement. This goes a long way in helping to look at the income side of things when you get ready to retire. In other words, what will be coming in!

Laundry detergent works the same in hot or cold water. It's true! Detergent is detergent, and the only difference is the temperature of water we wash in...hot or cold. Do as I do and wash as many of your clothes as you can in cold water. This will reduce the hot water heater from having to heat so much water.

> *Do as I do and wash as many of your clothes as you can in cold water.*

Maintain enough in your savings to cover 6 months of regular, everyday living expenses. If we take note of how much our regular living expenses are (mortgage, utilities, groceries, etc), we can come-up with a fairly accurate monthly amount. Once you have that number, multiply by six, and you pretty much have what you need to get by on should something suddenly happen like job loss, etc.

Never put a skillet, pot, or pan on a burner that is larger than the container you are heating. Placing a small cooking utensil on a big burner...electric or gas...wastes fuel.

Ovens are not to be used to warm or cook leftovers. God gave us microwaves so that we wouldn't have to heat the whole kitchen to warm-up a piece of pizza or cook tater tots. If you do need to warm up something especially in the winter, leave the oven door open after cooking and this will help warm the kitchen (be sure the oven is turned off, though!).

> *God gave us microwaves so...*

Purchase software that keeps track of how and where you spend your money. Now days, most computers come equipped with money management software. If so, set up and use it. If you happen to purchase a computer that does not have this kind of software, go out and buy it. They're not that expensive, and it will be well-worth the investment. If nothing else, keep track of your expenses with pen and paper. Excuse the pun, but be "religious" about posting and tracking your expenses. After only one month, you'll be shocked to discover where you've spent your money.

Quick access to vital records is a must, especially if there's been an accident. Having records like the amount of the deductible and the policy number of your house insurance, your health care desires as it deals with a feeding tube or ventilator, next of kin, or any special/ personal medical information is a must in times of confusion. <u>As a rule of thumb</u>: keep automobile insurance information in the glove box of your car, health care information with a friend or loved one, the people that need to be contacted first in the address book of your cell phone under "ICE" (In Case of Emergency), and any special medical needs in your wallet or purse.

Raise the deductible on your auto, health, and homeowner's insurance if you can swing it. You know as well as I that the lower the deductible, the higher your premiums. Conversely, the higher your deductible (the amount you will pay on an insurance claim before the insurance carrier will pay their portion) the lower your premiums. I have discovered that raising my deductible on my car and home insurance creates extra cash for me monthly. And what do I do with that extra cash…well, I put it in an interest-bearing savings account at my bank so that it's there should I need it to pay the deductible.

Save money by air-drying your dishes once the wash and rinse cycle is complete on your dishwasher. Again, every little bit helps, so turning the dial to "off" after the dishes are cleaned, opening the door to the dishwasher, and then letting the air in your house do the rest saves energy.

Tell your car insurer if you are driving less. Car insurance rates are based on several things including how far you drive to and from work. If you get a new job that is closer to your home than previously, be sure to report this to your car insurance carrier. The same thing may apply to car pooling or mass transportation. In addition, tell your carrier if someone comes off your policy like a student, that you park your car in a garage or under a carport and not on the street, and if your car has any extras like an ABS (anti-braking system), airbags, etc.

Use shades, blinds, and drapes inside your house to block the sun in the summertime and trees and shrubs outside to do the same. In addition to using white or light-colored curtains and shades, keep in mind that they need to be closed during the hottest part of each summer day. Blinds, especially, reflect the sun's rays away from the house. In wintertime, they can be opened to utilize all the sun's heating energy. As for trees and shrubs, it's best to plant them on the side of the house that gets the most summertime sun. As with shades, blinds, etc, it is wise to use them to block summertime rays. During winter, they help by blocking cold winds.

Vacuum coils of the major appliances like refrigerators, dishwashers, etc. This is no big deal. Simply get your vacuum out, hook-up the nozzle part, take off the metal or plastic piece around the bottom of the appliance, and go to town. Keeping the coils clean may help the appliance to work more efficiently and use less energy.

Watch-out that you're not getting too much withheld (from your taxes). A common mistake among people is that they get too much withheld from their salaries for tax purposes. In other words, they may be claiming several exemptions when they may be able to get by and have more money in their take-home checks by claiming fewer exemptions. Unlike my wife, I am not a CPA or a tax person, so this is one of those areas that you need to talk to an expert in this particular field.

X-amine your options to see if your bank has a service whereby they round your spending up to the nearest dollar and put that excess change into a savings account. I do this and it has proven to be a good thing. Here's how it works: I use my debit card to pay for something...let's say gas for the car...and the bill is $35.50. The bank then rounds that amount up to the nearest dollar...in this case, $36.00, takes the difference (50 cents) and deposits the 50 cents into my savings account. My bank even pays interest! In turn, I use what's accrued in my savings account to pay for the kid's college expenses like books, etc.

Yell at anybody in your house that you feel may be staying in the shower too long. I once read where showers use between ¼ and ½ of a home's water. Unless people in that home take cold showers, then that translates into the water heater having to work harder and longer. If yelling won't work, try using low-flow showerheads to possibly reduce the water and energy costs associated with showers.

Ziti, elbow macaroni, and other pastas are inexpensive and can be used to make countless kinds of dishes. Ask the chef or manager at your favorite Italian restaurant what food items cost the least but can easily be "dressed-up" and sold for a real profit and they will tell you pasta. There, I've done it...I've told you a little-known restaurant secret! And when pasta is purchased in bulk, the savings are even more outlandish. If Bubba were talking to Forrest Gump, he might say "there's spaghetti and meat sauce, spaghetti and meatballs, fettuccini Alfredo, penne, rigatoni,..."

Negotiating

I've heard it said all my life that there are two things in this world that are givens: *death and taxes*. However, I am quickly learning that even these two areas have some wiggle-room. For example, we will all die, yes. However, when we die is another area all together. Think about it. With feeding tubes, ventilators, and the absence of a living will, people can be kept alive indefinitely. As for taxes, it's the same thing. Not everybody pays taxes when they're supposed to. Some get caught and have to pay, while others work through bankruptcy lawyers to have their taxes reduced or all together eliminated (at least that's what those commercials say on TV).

My point is clear: *it seems that everything is negotiable*. More, death and taxes have shown us that there is a key to negotiating.

In the pages that follow, I take a look at the art of negotiating. Particularly, I want to share with you the art of *when* to negotiate, *how* to negotiate, and the likes. I do this in hopes that negotiating will help you become a better steward of your personal finances. In no particular order...

Do your homework. In other words, be on the look-out long before you need something. Next, check out the ads of the competitors, see what they're selling the (same) item for, and bring that ad with you to the store. Along the same line, be sure to watch for those in-store coupons. Is 20% off that one item in Store A really a bargain when compared to the same item in Store B?

<u>Case in point</u>: following my yearly physical, my doctor told me that my cholesterol was not what it should be considering my age, my exercise patterns, and my eating habits (either my LDL was too high or my HDL was too low...I can't remember exactly which it was). Subsequently, he asked that I give "serious thought" to taking a test called a CT Scan for Calcium Deposit. When I asked if my insurance covered it, I was told no. With that, I went about checking the cost for such a procedure. At the local hospital, it would be approximately $1,100.00. The larger hospital in the next town was going to charge me nearly $1,300.00. A short time later I called a private company that does this kind of thing in Raleigh, NC, (about 2 hours west of me), and their price: $350.00! The rewards of doing your homework.

BTW: I know you're concerned, so let me share

with you the results of that procedure. There was no calcium build-up, and I have a less than 1% chance of having a stroke. Anyway, I thought you might like to know.

This brings up another (medical) point about negotiating. Before the procedure, *ask if your health care provider offers a discount if you pay cash.* Paying cash means that the provider gets their money then and not 30 – 60 days later.

The best time to negotiate items such as cars, clothes, and other things is at *the end of the month or the quarter.* Car dealers are looking to reduce inventory and salespersons are looking to get a little extra in their paychecks. As for buying clothes and most other things, it's also at the end of the month when the account books are being closed or 6 – 8 weeks after items arrive (and the new things are beginning to arrive).

The best time to negotiate for something is when *the place is quiet and customers are at a minimum.* This way, you have the salesperson's undivided attention. The day to do this (see the chapter on Quick and Easy Things) is Thursday afternoons or evenings.

Be kind to the salesperson and call them by their first name (look at their nametag). Threatening to take your business to another store doesn't do anything but create animosity and ill feelings. As difficult as it may be, they're only doing their job and being nice never hurts!

Never find fault with the item. Saying that an item looks shabby or is overpriced starts things on a negative note. More, if it's cheaply made and overpriced, then why am I letting on that I want to buy it? Da!

Point out small flaws on the item and ask for a discount. Is a shirt missing a button? You can sew, right? A small scratch or dent on the side of a washing machine or dryer? I know it happens, but which of your family or friends asks to see the side of a washing machine or dryer? The two (washer and dryer) are usually placed side-by-side anyway!

Ask the salesperson's opinion. Ask them if this is the best deal you can get on the item? After telling them you have only so much money to spend, ask them if there is anything else you can (morally or ethically) do to get the item cheaper.

You will have more negotiating power if you plan to purchase several things instead of one thing. If you plan to buy a pair of pants, a shirt, and a tie, ask the salesperson if they will reduce the price of a belt.

If the sales person refuses to negotiate, *ask to see a manager.* As I once heard Oprah Winfrey say, "never talk to someone that tells you no that can't tell you yes in the first place."

Lastly, if you really want something, then *negotiate like you have nothing to lose...because you don't.* We negotiate because we want more, not less, right? So, if we lose, we're not out anything. I guess the key here is to act indifferent. If you don't get what you want, then walk away (and return to barter another day).

Outside Eating

As I sit down to write this chapter on "Outside Eating" (or eating out as most would call it), it's Monday morning. Looking back, my wife and I ate out three times over the weekend. On Friday night, we dined at our favorite Mexican place. We ate Saturday lunch at a fast food place. Yesterday, we took my wife's mother to a popular, nationally-recognized restaurant just off Interstate 40 (this explains why we had to wait 30 minutes...but it wasn't that bad, we rocked back-and-forth in those white, wicker rockers and played checkers until we heard those golden words, "Price, party of three, your table is now ready").

While eating out three times in three days may *not* seem like a big deal to most, it is to me! Growing-up, "eating out" meant sitting on the back porch with my brothers and sisters, around a hastily constructed dinner table, and enjoying whatever my mother had cooked that day. To actually sit down at a table and be served in a restaurant was something for the "upper crust." On those seldom occasions when we did go out and eat (which were few and far between), we would eat in a place that had orange, high-back booths, ripped seats, and a hook at the end of the booth to hang your coat. As for the food, it definitely overshadowed the ambiance.

Thirty years may have passed since I last sat down in a restaurant and had dinner with my mother, but a lot has changed in those thirty years. Despite the ever-increasing cost to eat-out, it seems that people are eating out more and more. Again, I ate out three times just this past weekend!

So what's the answer? Our schedules may be such that eating out is a growing and viable option, and yet we want to get the best "bang for our buck."   Fear not, because I have some suggestions for you on how to still enjoy eating out but not feel so guilt-ridden about the price that you're not able to enjoy the meal and the people you have sitting around the table with you. However, I ask that you remember that I'm a minister and teach at a college and not a nutritionist or a restaurant critic. Subsequently, my suggestions do not focus so much on what and how to eat as they do on when and where. As before, these are not only in alphabetical order but they also come fast and furious, so be ready...

Ask for a doggy bag. Hey, you paid for it so why not take home what you paid for. Many times, what you did not finish at the restaurant is a good start for a meal tomorrow.

Buffet all the way. While you can't take things home with you from a buffet, you can eat till you have to be rolled away. Just kidding! Buffets are an excellent way to not only have a variety of things to eat but also an excellent way to get much of your daily requirements of fruits, vegetables, proteins, etc. The key is to eat late...a late breakfast means a late lunch which may mean you don't feel like having dinner!

Choose from the child's menu instead of the adult one. Before you order, be sure to ask if you can do this.

Download coupons from the internet. Go to your favorite restaurant's website and see what's cookin'. Who knows, they may have a coupon on their website for your favorite dish and all you need to do to take advantage of the special is to simply download a coupon.

> **Eating out with a party, remember that the gratuity is usually included in the bill.**

Eating out with a party, remember that the gratuity is usually included in the bill. As such, there is no need to leave a tip...unless you want to!

Forget about ordering alcohol, sodas, or other drinks. Instead, you may want to consider ordering water with lemon. Ask someone in the restaurant business which items on the regular menu bring the biggest profits, and they will tell you that drinks bring a big return.

Go and eat during the "early bird" hours. The early bird hours are usually before the dinner rush hours...say 5:00pm. So, the key is to schedule your time so you arrive and are seated a few minutes before 5:00pm! Still, be sure to ask your waitperson if you made the "early bird" special.

Half meals. If you go to a restaurant and they give big portions, consider splitting the meal with someone at your table. <u>Caveat</u>: be sure to ask if there is any charge for an extra plate!

Inquire about any specials. When you enter a restaurant, look for any chalkboards or signs nearby that may list daily specials. As well, be sure to ask your waitperson.

Jot down where the special deals are and when they happen. If you like eating Mexican food, then make sure you not only know the night that the Mexican restaurant down the street offers two-for-one tacos but you also know the hours the special is held. Then, keep the list in plain sight...like on the refrigerator.

Kid's nights. Watch those newspapers, flyers, and billboards for kids' night.

Look for those vouchers...newspaper, TV, radio, or otherwise. One of the more popular and fastest growing trends among several restaurants are those vouchers that offer two-for-one meals, free appetizers, or $50.00 worth of dining vouchers for half-price. I've used these and they are great as gifts, but be sure to read the small print for any and all restrictions like when they can be used, what they can be used for, and when they must be used (the day of the week).

> ***...my wife says, you have Little Debbie Oatmeal pies and ice cream at home.***

Mondays are bad days to go out and eat. Why? To better manage costs, restaurants use food on a "first-in and first-out" basis. Simply put, anything left over from the weekend usually becomes Chef's Special on Monday. In addition, the last food deliveries are usually made on Friday or Saturday and this can mean that the food you ordered could (and I stress could) have been around for 2 or 3 days.

No desserts! We don't need to be purchasing them. Or, as my wife says, you have Little Debbie Oatmeal pies and ice cream at home.

Order an appetizer as a meal. Have you seen the size of some of the restaurant's appetizers lately? They are gigantic. Instead of ordering an entrée, consider getting an appetizer as it may cost less and be just as filling and delicious.

Pay with cash or a debit card. This will not only eliminate any lapses in memory but also get the cost of the meal out of the way. If you must pay by credit card, make sure the card pays you back in points, miles, or rewards.

Quiet places that are out of the way. Want a less-expensive yet tasty meal but do not want to come away suffering from sensory overload, then consider going to a quieter place just off the main drag. Many times, those places that have letters missing from their portable sign out-front or use an inverted number 5 for number 2, have excellent food at inexpensive prices.

Remember birthdays, etc. Many restaurants will give a person a free meal on their birthday. You may even try telling them it's your anniversary, you just graduated, or some other special occasion. Be careful, though, they may ask for a driver's license or some other form of identification that lists your birthday.

Senior discounts, or for that fact, any discount. Try as many as fits your particular situation, including AARP, military, student, whatever.

Take-out. If you can get something to go; I am convinced that we spend less money buying things we don't need like appetizers, drinks, and desserts.

Use those gifts cards. Like most, I simply forget to use gifts cards that I've been given for Christmas, etc., by members of the congregations I've served over the years. As a result, they expire. The solution is to use those gifts cards and pay strict attention to the expiration date on them. If you discover that you have one that's expired, go to the restaurant anyway, give it a shot, and negotiate. You never know!

Voice your request at the restaurant early on to have individual tickets. If there is one thing that miffs me more than bad service at a restaurant, it's wait-staff that automatically think that just because you're with a group everything is on one bill. Of course they want it on one bill, they get 12% - 18% gratuity. Ask for each person to pay their own bill and this will eliminate any misunderstandings between wait-staff and those that we are dining with at the restaurant.

Wait people are human beings, too. When she was needed for special occasions like banquets, weddings, and holidays, my mother worked at a small restaurant in my hometown for extra cash. As well, all three of my kids and I have also worked in the food service industry at one time or another in our lives. Personally, I could always tell which customers had waited tables earlier in their lives because they would generally clean-up after themselves, stack their plates, put all the silverware together, and leave a nice tip. So be kind and refined, because we never know the exact reason why a particular person is waiting on tables.

X-amine your bill carefully when you get it. Wait-people usually have anywhere from 5 – 7 tables to take care of on any given night. Add in the fact that it's Friday night, that one of those tables is a party of 6, and another of those tables has three kids in high-chairs and you have the possibility of error when it comes time to deliver the checks. As such, you could unknowingly get the check that says you had six steaks, six pieces of strawberry cheesecake, and two bottles of champagne, while the table next to you could get the check for two house salads and two waters. Don't laugh, it's happened!

Yoke special orders together to avoid paying extra. Let's say you and another person are out at a restaurant and both of you order something different. Sadly, there is something on your plate that you don't especially care for (like spinach) but the restaurant will not allow substitutes. The only way to get what you want is to order "ala carte." Before you go and pay extra to get a vegetable that you like, see if that other person likes spinach. If they do, then have them order a side that you like. When the entrees arrive, simply trade veggies!

Zoom in on meat and vegetables at the buffet and avoid the bread. When we eat bread with a meal, it tends to fill us up faster. If we eat enough bread, then we have little or no room to enjoy the other things that we paid for like a salad, vegetables, or meat. <u>Think about it</u>: what's the first thing that a wait-person brings you after they bring your drinks...a basket full of fresh, hot bread. Our automatic response is to eat bread and drink while the line to the buffet goes down. Consequently, there is a great chance that we will eat less and thus not get our money's worth.

Property

Stay with me now...My mother was born July 3, 1927, and graduated high school in the early summer of 1945. Shortly thereafter, she married. Some ten months later (April, 1946), she gave birth to the first of six children...a girl. In the fourteen years that followed, my mother would have five more children with the last one, a boy, born in October, 1960. It was not until the mid-1970's that she purchased her first home.

Located on Maple Avenue, the "new" house was a two-story structure covered with yellow aluminum siding, and it had both a front and back porch. Inside, the house had three bedrooms and one bath, all upstairs. The move from the "old" house...one that my mother rented from the local undertaker...was an easy one. The "old" house was three doors down the street from the "new" one! My mother (and the bank) bought the house from a former high school classmate of mine that was getting a divorce. I can't tell you much more than that about the house because most of the time I was away at school. Subsequently, I can't tell you what she paid for the house, if she made a down payment on the house, or how much her monthly house payment was. Sadly, she was only able to live in that house for five years. She died in January, 1979.

To summarize: my mother bought her first house when she was 47-years old, and compared to today's standards it was modest in size. Put another way, she paid rent for 29 of her 34 adult years!

What, you may ask, does all of this have to do with money management and becoming a good steward of personal finance? My answer: plenty! In one sense, owning a home can be one of the highlights and high-points of our lives. I'm sure it was for my mother. Owning a home makes a statement that our finances are such that we can afford a home and all the elements connected such as maintenance, upkeep, and paying taxes, and all at the same time that we're doing the normal things like paying bills and raising kids. What's one more thing on our plate, right?

However, homeownership is not without challenges. It takes time, money, and effort to keep a home from becoming a mere address on a street. Yes, calling a home our own takes work, it takes sacrifice, and it takes being good with money...much like my mother was. And that, my friend, is what this chapter is all about.

In a chapter of moderate length, I share with you some inexpensive, cost-effective things that can be done around our homes, particularly the outside, to make them something to be proud of. In one sense, many of these suggestions fall into the category of *preventative*...things that we need to do on a regular basis to keep our homes safe and livable. Conversely, I also share with you several simple things that can be done around the house to make it more *attractive*. Lest you forget, all of the advice I offer fits into the realm of saving you money in the long run. Once again, I am not an expert in this or any other area. Rather, these are some things that my mother did, things that others have done and shared with me, and things that I have done around my own home. In no particular order...

Make your January mortgage payment of the coming year in late December of the current year. This simple move will allow you to take the interest that you would have paid the following year and add it to your mortgage interest for the current year. Better yet, you can also add a little extra to each monthly mortgage payment (I divide my monthly mortgage payment by 12 and add that amount to each month's mortgage payment. By year's end, I've made thirteen payments instead of twelve). <u>Caveat</u>: the downside to paying the

January mortgage payment in December is that you will *not* be able to deduct it from next year's taxes.

Pay real estate taxes for the coming year in December of the current year. It's the same principle as above. If you're like me and choose to pay the taxes yourself instead of them coming out of your escrow account, paying them in December allows one to deduct them from taxes in the year they were paid. To take it one step further, educate yourself as to how your property taxes are assessed, when they are done, and how long between assessments. Who knows, maybe your place has been incorrectly assessed and you're paying more real estate taxes than you should.

If you have chosen to donate money or other items like furniture, clothing, etc, to organizations, do it before December 31. Once again, you can deduct these "offerings" from your taxes. However, be sure to get a receipt for your donation from the organization for your tax records.

Make your home easy to access from the outside. As a minister for nearly a quarter of a century, I have the honor of visiting quite a few homes. Some of these homes have been easy to get to...park the car, walk up to the door, and go in. On the other hand, I have visited just as many homes that required me to go through a jungle or an obstacle course in order to get to the front door!

Every year or two, have a full home inspection done by a qualified inspector. The more we live in a house, the more we may fail to notice little things that are happening around us. Torn screens on back doors, shutters that are old and faded, and small holes in the house's ductwork all may go unnoticed because they have developed slowly and we just never notice them. A home inspection may highlight these potential problems. In addition, a home inspection may also uncover unseen problems that could create major headaches.

Brush or wash down the exterior of your house (including windows, carports, and doors) on occasion. Where they come from or how they develop is beyond me, but I find cobwebs all over the exterior of my house...and not just in the summer. Use a broom on those places you can reach or use a water hose or power-washer for those hard-to-reach places. Doing this on a regular basis will deter bees and birds from building nests and other critters from making the exterior of your home their home.

As much as possible, regularly clean the exterior of major appliances. Like most other appliances around the house, refrigerators can quickly get a nasty build-up of dust around the coils. This goes for washers and dryers, dishwashers, and water-heaters. To help them run more efficiently and use less energy, vacuum around coils, vents, and any place in which large amounts of dust may accumulate. And while you're getting dusty and dirty, change the air filters for the furnace and the air conditioner.

Clear-out any weeds or roots around the house that have the potential to grow and create problems. Tree roots that go unchecked can cause serious damage to a home's foundation. Likewise, vines that are allowed to grow without recourse have been known to pull mortar from the bricks and wrap around air conditioner units. Consequently, this causes the A/C unit to work harder and use more energy. Finally, trim tree limbs so that they do not interfere with utility lines or rub against shingles every time the wind blows. If left unchecked, limbs can rip and tear roofing materials. Unsure about what to cut and how, call an expert in the tree business.

Watch for drips under kitchen and bathroom cabinets and around the toilet. It may be sweating pipes, but if the water continues to drip it may signal a more serious problem.

Make it a regular practice to clean leaves off the roof and out of gutters and downspouts. This is another of those hidden things that can cause serious problems for a homeowner. Allowing leaves to accumulate on the roof can create a makeshift dam that stops water from flowing. When water backs-up, it has to go somewhere, right? If allowed to dam-up and stand, water will eventually find its way into the attic and beyond. The same applies to gutters and downspouts. Every few months (more during the fall months), get a ladder and get on the roof. Clean out those gutters. It may be a dirty job, but you can pay now or pay later. Lastly, turn the water-hose on and let it run down those downspouts for a few minutes. You may be surprised at what comes out.

> *Make it a regular practice to clean leaves off the roof and out of the gutters and downspouts.*

If you have storm windows, make sure they are closed (and stayed closed). Storm windows are there for a purpose...added protection from excessive heat loss. A simple walk around the exterior of the house will give you an answer if all the storm windows are down. While you're at it, make a list of the things that need to be done. Then, you can do as I do. I write each job down on a piece of paper and put the piece of paper in a container. On those occasions when I have time to do things around the house, I go, stick my hand in the container, and pull out a job. I know, I know...it's funny, but it works.

Fix any water drips. While a slow but continuous drip may seem insignificant, remember this: it doesn't take but a few drips to fill-up a spoon, it takes only a few spoonfuls of water to fill-up a small container, it only takes a few containers to fill-up a pitcher, and it only takes a few pitchers to fill-up a gallon. And if more than one faucet is dripping, you're paying for more water than you're actually using! And if you hear the toilet filling up even though no one has flushed it, it means it too is losing water.

Looking to add a brick border around the flower gardens, consider your city's solid waste yard. People and businesses are remodeling and cleaning-out all the time. I once knew a man that went to a builder that was constructing a brick home nearby and asked if he could have any extra brick. The man came away with so many that he built himself a barbeque pit.

Educate yourself about whatever you're going to plant. In addition to knowing if that boxwood you're wanting to plant in the front of the house needs a lot of sun or a little, you also need to know how big it will get and how fast it will grow. Otherwise, you may be spending more time planting and re-planting because the bush keeps dying. Worse yet, you may come home one day and find the roots of that pine tree you planted 5-years ago has grown into your sewer lines.

Time your purchases, inside and out. A little confused when you should buy and plant grass? How about when to buy major appliances? If so, jump ahead to the next chapter in this work entitled: Q: quick and easy things.

Divide and conquer. Completing a major program in phases not only allows you to evaluate your progress and adjust as needed, but it's also a lot easier on the pocketbook. As well, this may save on overall costs...little charges instead of one big one may help you avoid purchasing things you do not need.

Look for plants that use very little water. Not only will you save on your water bill, but you will not have to plan your daily calendar around watering plants two or more times a day. You may want to develop a system to collect water from your roof.

Do not cover-up air (exchange) vents with carpet or furniture. This is one of those you probably already know, right? Just checking.

Make a monthly list of when things need to be done around the house. I have one of those black, 3-ring notebooks with 12 pages in it...one for each month of the year. The first page is January, and on that page I have written all the things I need to do around the house in the month of January. The next page is February, and so on.

I change batteries in the smoke detectors whenever the clocks are changed. Specifically, I change the batteries when we set the clocks ahead one hour (in the spring) and again when we change clocks back one hour in the fall.

Quick and Easy Things

In this chapter, I want to share with you some little things that can save you big bucks. A vast majority of these suggestions come from personal experience. Then again, just as many come from things I saw my mother do and things I've seen (and heard) the members of the congregations I've served do as they endeavored to become better stewards and managers of their personal finances.

To make things simple and to keep with the overall structure of this work, I've not only put these suggestions into two columns: *item* and *when to buy*, but (once again) I've also alphabetized them. Whenever possible, I've also included a *brief explanation of why that time is best to buy*.

Finally, let me say this. The list is not an exhaustive one by any means. Neither time nor space allows me to list every category or when might be the best time to purchase that particular item. I move through this list quite rapidly because you do not need to know so much "why" as you need to know "when and how."

With that, we're off to the races (as they say)…

Item	When to buy/ How to
Air Conditioner	October– January
Bulbs (light)	Whenever needed, but be sure to purchase compact fluorescent ones instead of the old incandescent ones. The fluorescent ones may cost more, but in the long-run they will save you money and last longer.
Clothes	Wait for the off-season (winter to buy fall, spring to buy winter, etc). I have found that the best time to buy is Thursday afternoon or evenings, approx. 6 – 8 weeks after items arrive in the stores.
Dishes/ Cookware	Late-spring and late-fall.
Electronics	For TV's, the best time is definitely January and maybe March. If possible, I wait to buy a computer until August and the tax-free weekend. However, don't rule- out Black Friday (the day after Thanksgiving) or Cyber Monday (the Monday after Black Friday).

Flea Market   Late in the day. However, remember to go early in the day to check-out what's there. When you return, bring only small bills with you.

Garden   August. Many of the plants will be
(and yard)   root-bound by now and garden centers are looking to unload as much of their seasonal stock (including mowers, patio furniture, etc.) as possible.

Home   For the big appliances such as
appliances   washers and dryers, refrigerators, etc, the months of September, October and January. However, watch for mid-year specials around Memorial Day and July 4th. Small appliances: December and January. Also buy appliances that are Energy Star rated because it will save on utilities and also give you a tax break.

Industrial   Industrial tools
tools   Anytime...of course, I'm a guy and we can never have too many!

Jewelry   The only advice that I can offer here is to avoid buying around the "big" days like the holidays, Mother's Day, and Valentine's Day. Watch for sales!

Kids toys   Fall, preferably October and November...before Thanksgiving.

Leisure (bikes, etc)   January and February for bikes. As for other outdoor things like boats, sports and camping equipment, etc, early in the year or just after the season ends.

Mattresses   Probably May; however, buy when you need it. Still, look for one that's comfortable for you, durable, and within your price range. By all means, make sure it's delivered, set-up is free, and the store will take and dispose of the old one. You may even want to ask for a free frame!

New tires   This is a no brainer! When the old ones begin showing wear is the best time to begin thinking about buying new ones. Safety is paramount.

Outdoor appliances	Once again, the best time to buy is after the season ends (i.e. outdoor grills in the fall).
Property	A biggie! Ask any realtor and the answer is always "now." Still, you have to go with what works for you.
Quirky	<u>Halloween costumes</u>: November 1; <u>Wrapping paper</u>: January; <u>Plastic, Pink flamingoes</u>: anytime (but you'll have to replace them the day after you put them out).
Restaurant	Definitely not dinner on Mondays because that's when most restaurants serve their version of "chef's surprise" (aka the weekend leftovers). Here, you need to do your homework such as looking on-line for menus that fit your taste and budget, early bird specials, and discounts. As well, keep an eye-out for BOGO meals, coupons, and special promotions. When traveling, I like to go to a place around late morning that has a breakfast buffet and eat two meals in one sitting. Hey, don't laugh…it saves money on meals!

Sheets and linens	Most definitely it's January and that's that!
Travel	Once more, a great deal depends on schedule and personal finance. For particulars, go back to the chapter on "F: flying."
Undergrad. things	Individuals enrolled in college need just about everything from textbooks to supplies and transportation. <u>Textbooks</u>: go on-line or watch for lists of books to be sold and posted on bulletin boards near the various school departments (Psychology books near the Psychology Dept). <u>Supplies</u>: whenever they're on sale so don't confine yourself to those semi-annual, tax-free, weekends. <u>Transportation</u>: I still encourage my kids to use public and university transportation. After all, I pay for it through federal, state, and local taxes, and they pay for it in their university fees!

Vehicles	Although I covered a great deal of this in a previous chapter (A: Automobiles), a few points bear repeating such as buying at the end of the month or quarter buying, in September, and going into the dealership with a good idea of what you want to buy (model) and how much car you can afford.
Water heaters	When you need one you need one and waiting for the best time to buy is not an option. Still, cutting shower time and reducing the setting on the water heater to 120 degrees can save you hundreds of dollars each year in utilities costs.
X-scape (OK, this is a stretch)	Again, I offered my ideas on this in a chapter (F: flying) and in the chapter (R: road trips) and I don't want to beat a dead horse!
Yellow Squash Zucchini, etc.	I'm talking fresh and locally grown, of course! The best time is during the summer months and just before the person selling the stuff calls it a day (just like the Flea Market). For more specifics, go to the chapter labeled G: Groceries.

Road Trips

As I sit down to write this chapter, my wife and I have just put the final touches on a weekend trip. We will fly to Pittsburgh on Friday afternoon. After landing, we will pick-up a rental car and drive to the hotel we have reserved for the night. On Saturday, we will drive to West Virginia to take part in a fall tradition that goes back decades and includes beers, cheers, and the Mountaineers. You guessed it...we will be attending a WVU football game. Following the game, we will get in our rental car and head west on Route 7 toward good, old New Martinsville. We are scheduled to stay in one of the few hotels located in town. The next day we will visit with brothers and sisters and anybody else that wants to stop by and say hello. Our returning flight is scheduled to depart late afternoon and we should be home by the time the 10:00pm news comes on.

I share this with you because our planned weekend and this chapter have a common theme;

namely, "road trip." And as we draw nearer to the end of the alphabet, we draw nearer and nearer to the end of this work. Accordingly, it would be bad etiquette for me *not* to say something about how to save money on road trips. In an earlier chapter (the chapter entitled F: Flying), you discovered not only the best day and time to fly but also the best way to get the best price on an airline ticket. Since you remember these "flying" tips, there is no need to repeat them. You do remember, right?

Now, I want to share with you some easy, cost-effective, money-saving ways to take a road trip. Specifically, I want to share with you how to save money as you travel while getting some deals on car rentals and hotels and several things in-between. I may stray "outside the lines" here, but don't fear...I'm a good driver and even better with money.

> *...it would be bad etiquette for me not to say something about how to save money on road trips.*

Want a good alternative to flying, then try the train. Riding the train may not be as fast as flying nor will you get to your destination as quickly as driving, but traveling by train can be a whole lot less-expensive and not nearly as stressful. In addition, you get to see things that one usually wouldn't see from a plane or car window. Train routes go through major cities and small towns, over flatlands and through mountain passes, and all the while taking us places that are not found in travel guides and brochures. Once again, traveling by train reminds us that it's not so much about the destination as it is the journey. If you want to see even more and have the time, take the bus.

Be sure you stop at the visitor's center or state rest stop and ask about any discounts on hotels, restaurants, or attractions. Go to the front desk, ask questions, and see what they have for free. As you leave, be sure to look around for those magazine racks that offer discounts on hotel rooms.

Go on-line and search for any cultural, athletic, or civic events in the towns you'll be traveling through. Being in love with baseball as I am, the first thing I do when I know that we are traveling through a certain city is to see if they have a minor league baseball team. If they do, I find out if the team is in town and if they are playing any home games during that time. If they are, you can bet I'll be there since this is some of the best entertainment for the price. You just can't beat admission tickets, 2 hot dogs, 2 drinks, and one bag of peanuts for less than $20.00. For other cities large and small, you can get a map and take a free walking tour, see a parade or stroll through a street fair, and just about anything else. The more research you do the better the results.

If the restaurant prices are too high, go to the local grocery store, buy a pre-made sandwich, and sit by the water. Where we live in Washington is one of the most beautiful places in eastern North Carolina...if not the eastern U.S. What makes it so beautiful is the Pamlico River. Morning, noon, or night, it is not uncommon to see countless people from every walk of life enjoying the outdoors. Some are just sitting and watching and others are sitting and eating. Whatever the case, it's all free...except for the sandwich, of course!

Don't just travel in the summer. Visiting the out-of-the-way places during the off-seasons may get you hearty discounts and a great deal of attention from the local staff you may not get during the peak travel season.

Visiting travel sites is a good place to comparative shop, but don't forget to go to the websites of hotels and car rental companies. Granted, the national travel websites allow you to compare prices, amenities, and even read reviews, but they do not always have the best prices. Instead, call the hotel or car rental place directly and ask about any discounts or specials. Tell them you really like their location, their service, and that you want to stay there but the price is a little too high. Is there anything they can suggest? Yes, ask for any discounts, and by all means, negotiate.

Review your auto insurance policy and see if you can decline the car rental insurance. This amount alone increases the charge on most rentals by several dollars a day. Before you say yes to the extra charge, do your homework and check-out your policy.

Take a long, hard look at the interior and exterior condition of your rental car. Before you get in the driver's seat and drive off, walk around the car with the rental agent and draw attention to any scratches, dings, or rips that you see. If they are not highlighted before you drive-off, you may have to pay for them when you return the car. After all, the rental place will not know if the marks were there before or if they were made while the car was in your possession.

Be careful eating or drinking things out of those hotel mini-bars. Hotels charge for everything you use that comes from for those refrigerators. Even worse, you could be paying $3.00 or $4.00 for a bottle of water that costs you 99 cents at the Rite-Aid next door.

Book hotels that provide a free breakfast. I have stayed in some hotels where the breakfast bar is nothing but coffee and doughnuts. This is especially disheartening since I don't drink coffee! On the other hand, I have stayed at hotels where the breakfast bar is a feast that includes waffles, cereal, bagels, boiled eggs, and 3 kinds of juice. When booking a room, ask about the breakfast bar.

> *...you could be paying $3 or $4 for a bottle of water that costs 99 cents at the Rite-Aid next door.*

If possible, stay in a room or rent a car that rewards you. If the hotel gives you points on your frequent flyer award, book it. If the car rental place does the same, book it. If you charge the room and the car with a credit card that gives you flyer miles, then you have definitely died and gone to heaven!

Enroll in a hotel loyalty program. Most, if not all, of the major hotel chains have some kind of loyalty program whereby they reward you for staying with them. To get into the program, simply ask the front desk person. If you travel a great deal, the points, discounts, and prizes add-up quickly.

If traveling by car, go on-line and check-out the local gas prices in the cities you'll be passing through or are visiting. Doing your homework may mean paying considerably less for a gallon of gas at a particular station even though it's a little further to drive.

Don't forget that you have a friend with AAA. One of the wisest things I've ever done...I took out membership some ten years ago and it's paid for itself a hundred times over.

Service Stations

If you were to ask my siblings to rank *my* knowledge of mechanical things on a scale of 1 – 10 (1 being no knowledge and 10 being an expert), they would tell you that the depth and degree of my knowledge of mechanical things would "hover" around *negative 5*. Until just a few years ago, they were convinced that I thought there was such a thing as a left-handed screwdriver!

The truth is I know more than they think I know about cars, electricity, plumbing, and other everyday things. Yes, I've experienced a great number of situations since that January day in 1955, and each has broadened my base of knowledge about how things operate. So, if you ever meet my three brothers and two sisters, go along with their not-so-glowing comments about my lack of knowledge of how things work. After all, I have an image to keep up.

One of those areas that I've learned about over the past several years is the in's-and-out's of how service stations operate. You know those places that sit on just about every corner in America. In addition to supplying gas, they work on cars, sell food, and offer advice (most commonly, how I'm not properly taking care of my car by doing the regular maintenance on it!). Again, the truth is that it's getting done but maybe not at their place. Again, that's between you and me, right?

In this chapter, I want to share with you some ways to minimize your trips to the local service station, while at the same time reducing your expenses. Again, my goal is to help you become a better steward and money manager of your personal finances. That said, let's put the pedal to the metal (excuse the pun)...

Do your homework about a station or a mechanic. Ask anyone that operates a reputable business and they will tell you that honesty and integrity are the cornerstones on which good businesses are built. The same thing applies to where you take your car for maintenance and repairs. Stations want your business and they will do all they can to keep you. To find such a place, ask family, friends, and neighbors who they take their car to when things are not just right. Similarly, ask people who drive the same kind of car as you where they go. Finally, be sure to remember that if you take your car to a mechanic a few times to let them work on it and you're not happy with the results, you can always take your business elsewhere.

Not all people that operate stations are mechanics. In most areas, the days of a truly qualified mechanic are gone. The reason is that most stations are more profitable and experience less headaches selling beer, bread, and bubble gum than repairing ball joints, bulbs, and bearings. It all boils down to two aspects: volume and overhead. Rather than having to pay a mechanic to do a repair that may take hours or days, a station can make just as much money (and maybe more) in less time selling small things that people want and need.

> *Buy what you absolutely, positively need...and get the rest some other place.*

Avoid buying those big ticket items at service stations. This advice applies in a number of areas. Don't buy tires at a service station, because the mark-up is usually horrendous. Likewise, and if you can avoid it, don't buy a gallon of milk, a loaf of bread, or those regular grocery items because it's the same thing...high mark-up. You come in to pay for the gas, and then you think to yourself, "hey, I'm thirsty." So, you go and buy a soda that costs

$1.39 there and 99 cents at the Food Lion next door. As you stand in line, you think to yourself, "hey, I need some chips to go with my soda." So, you grab a bag of chips that normally cost you $1.29 at Kroger but you'll be paying $1.59 for them here. Finally, you need some dessert, so you grab a Snickers bar. Forget about buying the smaller, 79 cent size. The station only has the jumbo bar that costs twice as much and can feed a small army! <u>Bottom line</u>: buy what you absolutely, positively need at the service station and get the rest some other place.

Do your transaction at the pump. Why? See above. If you don't go inside, you won't be tempted to buy things that you don't need like those white, Styrofoam coolers that cost $5.99 at the service station and half that at Wal-Mart.

Shop around for gas. I have found that gas prices at stations that are located near interstates can be several cents more a gallon than stations located at that same exit but a mile or less down the road. Don't go driving around to find the least expensive gas, though, you'll only use up the savings that you may have earned by going to that station down the road. Instead, watch for signs as you near the exit of the interstate. They'll tell you what's around and how far it is off the exit. Around town, the best advice for getting the least expensive gas is to go on-line or pay attention as you drive.

Don't even think about applying for or using a (gas) company card. The interest rates that companies charge on gas cards may far exceed the rate on some of your highest credit cards. Be late or miss one payment and your rate may surely increase. <u>Do as I do</u>: use the gas company cards sparingly, pay the bill immediately after it arrives, and, by all means, do not charge repairs or parts on the card unless you're going to pay them by the due time. Yes, it's OK to use your personal credit card, especially if you can get points and pay the bill on time, but use that gas company card in moderation.

When you can, do the small maintenance things yourself. On several occasions, I have changed my own oil and replaced bulbs, batteries, and filters. Yes, my dear brothers and sisters, I did it myself! Other times, I have let the service station do it. Hey, I do what I can to keep the economy going and job losses to a minimum. If you want to learn how to do it, first read up on it via a reference book from the library or on-line. Then, you may want to consider signing-up to be a part of a course at the local college or technical school on basic car maintenance. When you're ready, I recommend that you then ask someone to come and supervise as you do it the first few times. As well, it doesn't take the skills of a rocket scientist to check the coolant/anti-freeze in the radiator and fill if needed; make sure the tires are inflated to the right pressure; make sure the brake fluid is filled; or check for holes or cracks on hoses, belts, or the blades of your windshield wipers.

Watch for coupons in the mail and newspapers, and remember a trade school may be nearby. Again, businesses want your business, and one of the ways to do that is by offering discount (coupons) for certain services. <u>Caveat emptor</u>: be sure to read the small print in the ad completely because some stations will offer some astronomically-low price for an oil change. However, they fail to tell you that the price is for "labor only" and does not include parts such as oil and oil filters. If you have a dent or need brakes or a tune-up, check to see if there is a local trade school in your area. As with any trade school, the work is usually done by novices but they are supervised by well-trained and quite knowledgeable teachers.

Give serious consideration to how often you change your oil. I've heard it said, and I agree, that many factors go into deciding how often the oil needs to be changed in a car. Some will say that the oil needs to be changed every 3,000 miles. I disagree, but then again, I'm no expert. I tend to think that the age of a car, how the car is driven (city driving, long distance, etc.) and overall driving conditions (specifically, the weather) determine how often the oil is changed. In addition, I firmly believe that the newer technology of both today's cars and the oil itself allows the time between changes to be longer than most believe. As for me, I go about 5,000 - 7,500 miles between oil changes.

Fight the temptation to get your car washed each time you fill-up. At the local places around my town, the cost to wash a car at the same place it's filled-up with gas varies

> *Fight the temptation to get your car washed each time you fill-up.*

anywhere from $5.00 to $8.00. If I wash my car every time I fill it up with gas (which is about once a week) and pay for the best option (the one with wax and under-spray), I could end-up paying well over $400.00 a year for car washes alone! If you are the kind of person that washes your car each week, then I recommend that you wash your car at home because it's a lot less expensive. However, if you live in an area where the weather dictates that salt or other agents are spread on the road to help improve driving conditions, then by all means get those car washes as often you feel you need them.

Finally, *compose a schedule for regular maintenance, keep a log of what's been done and when it was done, and try to follow the owner's manual.* Volvo owners are notorious for this. We know when the oil was changed last, when the brakes were changed last, and so on. Your regular mechanic should have your car's records on a database, but just in case, it is good for you keep one as well.

You can always improve the bottom line on car expenses by *changing your driving habits* (no rabbit starts, using the cruise control on the open road, removing unwanted and unnecessary items from your trunk, not allowing your car to sit and idle for prolonged periods of time), *driving a car that costs less to operate, using mass transportation, carpooling, biking, or walking.* All of these help to reduce your expenses. Driving a more financially efficient car means driving one that saves you money because it takes less to operate it on a daily basis or to repair. Many times, mass transportation costs less, gets us there faster, and with less hassle (especially if we have to find a parking place). With carpooling, it's a flat fee and many costs are shared. As for biking and walking, we're not only getting physically fit but we're also doing our part for the environment, cutting down on traffic congestion, and (possibly) reducing auto insurance rates by doing less driving.

Telephone

A young businessman rented a beautiful office and furnished it with antiques. However, no business was coming in. Sitting there, worrying, he saw a man come into the outer office. Wanting to look busy, he picked up the phone and pretended he was negotiating a big deal. He spoke loudly about big figures and huge commitments. Finally, he put down the phone and asked the visitor "Can I help you?"

The man said, "I've come to install the phone." Telephones...they are the bane of my existence. Everywhere we look, there is a telephone, especially cell phones. I know they are important in our lives, but why does one need a cell phone strapped to their side when they arrive on Sunday mornings for worship? The only one they need to be talking with at that time is the Almighty!

Even more irritating is how much people overpay for a phone and related services. Does one really need to have more than one phone? Does a person really need to have all those bells and whistles?   In this chapter, I share with you some ways to reduce your phone bills but still be able to impress people by not only having all that you need in the way of services but also doing it for less.

> ## If you have a cell phone, then get rid of that landline.

If you have a cell phone, then get rid of that landline. Why have 2 lines and 2 service contracts...a cell phone and a landline...especially if you take your cell phone everywhere you go. You realize you're pretty much paying double for one service when you have a cell phone and a landline, right?

Be sure to get a (cell) phone plan that allows you free nights and weekends. By all means, know the terms of your contract (i.e. when does "night begin"...6:00pm, 7:00pm, etc, and when does the "weekend" begin and end...Friday, 6:00pm until Sunday, 11:59pm?).

If you're looking at a cell phone contract, then consider a family plan with some restrictions. With us older people talking more and more on our cell phones and with our kids "texting" more and more, consider a plan with unlimited minutes but with limited texts.

Consider a pay-as-you-go or pre-paid phone. If you want to keep your landline but still want all the freedom of a cell phone, then consider a phone plan that allows you to put a certain amount of minutes on a cell phone and then use as needed. Basically, you get a cell phone number and some minor services. <u>Caveat</u>: be careful who gets your cell number. Incoming and outgoing minutes add-up quickly.

Do you really need all those extras on your landline? If you really don't need them, then why pay for all those extras like caller ID, call waiting, etc?

Examine your bills carefully. Just the other day, I took a look at my monthly cell phone bill and noticed a charge for $3.99. When I called the phone company, they said it was insurance on my phone should I drop it or if it is stolen. I told them to remove it immediately. Afterwards, I got to thinking…how long has that been on there? Turns out, I have been paying that $3.99 for 4 months! How it got on there in the first place I'll never know.

If you plan on traveling and your cell phone charges for roaming, then consider a calling card. In addition to saving you money, a calling card reduces the worry over keeping track of a cell phone since it fits quite easily into a wallet, small purse, or your pocket. However, be familiar with the terms, restrictions, and charges for using a calling card (i.e. so many units/minutes come off the card when using a public phone to make a call).

Consider SKYPE or Magic Jack. These are two great ways to save on long-distance calls. With *SKYPE,* you chat with other *SKYPE* users via your computer for free. Yes, free! For non-computer chats with people on landlines, there is a minimal cost but it's still less than paying for a landline. With the *Magic Jack,* you pay for the "jack" itself that simply plugs into your computer and a small yearly fee. Again, it's less than paying long-distance for a landline.

> *...any (services) you can do without.*

Call your phone carrier (landline or cell), ask them what services you currently have, and if there are any you can do without. Be honest, tell them you're trying to reduce your phone charges, and see if they have any suggestions. You may be paying for services you neither know you have nor want.

Shop around. Again know your plan and what you have, know what you want, and see which company can give you the best rate. Don't worry about changing phone numbers...most companies allow you to take your old number with you.

Consider your needs. Some people need a landline because they run a business out of their home. Other people need a landline because that's how they get the internet. Still, other people want a landline because they do not want to give-out their cell number. <u>Bottom line</u>: evaluate your needs on a regular basis and see if there have been any recent changes that allow you to change or reduce services and features.

Utilities

Like several other chapters in this work, the tips that I could offer on how to reduce your utility costs may easily fill an encyclopedia. Even then, I would not have covered everything! I definitely don't want to produce something this lengthy and (for sure) you don't want to read something like this. With that in mind, I want to share with you twenty-six of what I feel are the most energy-efficient and money-savings things that can be done to reduce utility bills. More, I've listed those suggestions in alphabetical order.

Hopefully, some of the things I've listed you're already doing in your home. If so, good for you! If you find a suggestion that you are *not* doing, give it a try because you never know.

With that, onward and upward toward saving money and becoming a better steward of what we already have...

Analyze your heating and air conditioning bills to see if a programmable thermostat would save you money. An adjustable thermostat allows you to set a schedule of when the heating or air conditioning should come-on and go-off. This will save money especially when no one is at home, at nighttime when most are asleep, or when we leave and forget to turn them off.

Bundle services (cable, telephone, and internet) for a lower price. If you have all three of these services with the same company, ask about a discount for bundling them together. In addition to paying just one bill, you have to call only one company should problems (technical or otherwise) arise.

Cut luxury items that you do not need. Do you really need 500 TV channels? Do you really need a landline phone in light of the fact you use your cell phone more and more? Do you really need HBO and Showtime? If the answer to these and others questions is no, then consider cutting some services and reducing others. After all, you can only watch one channel at a time and talk to one person at a time! If you still want to trim expenses, then drop the cable completely.

Delay some indoor chores until later in the day. Why operate the dryer at the same time the air conditioner is running? Why heat the oven to bake in the middle of the day? These and other related chores create unnecessary heat in your home, especially during the summer months. This is a great reason to quit doing those chores around your home during the daylight hours between May and September.

Energy-efficient appliances save more money than we think. If it's time for some new appliances (like it is for us), you can bet that appliances we buy will be energy-efficient and have the Energy Star logo on them. Products stamped with the Energy Star meet or exceed standards set by the Department of Energy and all but guarantee to reduce energy use by as much as 30%.

Fluorescent bulbs are a big money-saver. It's a widely known fact that replacing incandescent bulbs with fluorescent ones not only saves money in the long run, but they also last longer than incandescent bulbs while producing the same amount of light but use significantly less energy and put off less heat. More, the savings will pay for the bulbs in no time.

Go ahead and adjust that heating and air conditioning a few degrees up or down. Most utility people will tell you that raising the thermostat setting 2 or 3 degrees in summer and lowering it the same in winter will save money, and I agree. In summer, I put my thermostat between 77 – 79 degrees and 63 – 65 in winter. The energy savings have been more than I ever expected.

Have an inspection done to see if you need additional insulation in the attic. If there is one thing that can be done that will save a homeowner the most money on utility bills while at the same time be the least expensive to do, it has to be this one! Either rolled or blown in, insulation with at least an R-30 rating is a must for all homes. While you're at it, don't forget to insulate around the pull-down stairs. To see if there is a leak

> *If you see the light, then your money is going up, up, and away!*

around the stairs, simply turn on the attic light, close the pull-down stairs, and look-up. If you see light, your money is going up, up, and away.

Insulate your water heater. Next to one or two other appliances, the water heater is next in line for the most energy consumption. Wrapping the heater with an insulated "blanket" can save additional money on utility bills particularly if your heater is more than 10 years old. If you decide to wrap a gas heater, be doubly careful not to block any vents, etc.

Just putting on a light sweater or wrapping-up in a blanket while watching TV in the winter means that you can lower your thermostat a few degrees. Go ahead, and try it. You'll find that it works.

Kindly ask your service provider if they would be willing to offer any discounts in order to keep you as a customer. To begin the process, simply call the cable or telephone people (this will probably not work with utility providers since they are possibly the area's sole provider) and tell them that you are trimming your budget and may have to cut or reduce services. If at first they say no, then be persistent. Explain to them that you have been a faithful customer and (hopefully) have always paid your bills on time. To keep you as a customer, they will most likely go through several options with you including reducing your current plan (from getting 500 channels to the basic package) or signing up or extending an agreement to stay with them for 2 or 3 years. Above all, be kind and avoid threatening to take your business elsewhere. Remember, they may have the only horse in town!

Line around exterior doors with weather-stripping. An extremely high amount of heating and cooling is lost as a result of cracks in doors and windows. In addition, be sure that the fireplace damper is closed when not in use. <u>Caveat</u>: weather-stripping is just as important in the summer as it is in the winter. Besides, the weather-stripping is inexpensive and easy to install.

Make a call to your local electric/utility company and see if they will do an energy audit. Performed by qualified engineers, these audits are free and last about 90 minutes. When completed, the homeowner has a written list of several things they can do to make the home more energy efficient. I had one done and the minor suggestions have reduced my monthly electric bill.

> ***When completed, the homeowner will have a written list of several things they can do to make the home more energy efficient.***

Never forget to check the lint screen on your dryer. In addition to becoming dangerous, lint build-up can cause your dryer to work longer and harder.

Open the back door, go outside, and hang laundry on the clothesline especially heavy items like throw rugs and beach towels. Heavy items like these take longer to dry using a dryer. Subsequently, the dryer must run longer and use more energy. On second thought, does that towel need to be washed and dried at all since you only used it to dry off?

Pull the plug on those things around the house that you use only occasionally. Appliances like fax machines, printers, DVR machines, VCR's, computers, and the like that have a clock on them should be unplugged if at all possible. If anything, plug them all into a power strip so that they can be all turned off at once. And while you're at it, do you really need that old refrigerator in the garage running and half-full of items since you purchased that new, more energy-efficient one? Finally, try to use your laptop on a hard, flat surface instead of a plusher one. Using the laptop as it sits on a carpeted floor can not only block airflow but also make the computer work harder...using more energy. <u>Bottom line</u>: even though they're plugged in, some appliances use energy even when they're off! Hey, every penny helps.

Quit opening the door to the oven to check on cooking food. Set a timer, close the door, and leave it shut until the timer goes off. Each time the oven door is opened, it loses heat.

Regular maintenance on the furnace and air conditioning units is a must. Beyond having the units serviced prior to every season (furnaces in the fall and air conditioners in the spring), get in the habit of changing filters frequently. Most filters cost only a few dollars each, but when changed on a regular basis can save lots of money.

Shorter showers save money. If you can't take shorter showers, then purchase a low-flow shower-head. You'll be amazed how such a simple move can save you money.

Temperature on the water-heater should be approximately 120 degrees. You don't need it any hotter than that because this is adequate for safely cleaning dishes and enjoying comfortable showers! Besides, I understand that for every 10 degrees the water-heater is reduced means a 3 – 5% savings on your electric bill.

Understand the methods to get the most out of your ceiling fans. In addition to making sure the fans have multiple settings for speed and the blades are big enough to do the job, be sure to remember that the blades on the fan should be moving in counter-clockwise during summer. In winter, the blades should be moving in a clockwise direction.

Vent your dryer so that the hose (eventually) ends-up outside. Otherwise, the hot air from the exhaust may cause your air conditioning unit to work harder.

Wash clothes in cold water whenever possible. Doing this reduces the need for your water-heater to work and thus reduces energy needed to heat the water. And while we're talking about the washer, be sure to wash only full loads.

X-amine to make sure lamps, TV's, and other appliances are not placed near thermostats. They give off heat and heat will make your cooling unit run longer and more often.

Yellow or similar colored (like white) shades, blinds, and curtains help reflect the sun's rays during summer months. In turn, this keeps the inside of the house cooler and decreases the amount of time the air conditioner needs to run. Of course, those same shades, blinds, and curtains need to be opened during the winter months to allow as much sunlight into the house as possible to help with heating.

Zip over to your local utility provider. A new program beginning to make its rounds in several parts of the U.S. is one whereby a household signs-up to have a home's heating or air conditioning shut-off electronically by the utility provider for a few minutes during peak-usage times during the weekdays. During peak/demand times, you know as well as I that energy charges increase dramatically. This new feature may prove quite helpful since most people are usually not at home during the peak/demand time (2:00 – 4:00pm). Besides, the shut-off usually lasts for 15 minutes or so during those two hours.

Visiting Other Countries

In this day and time, it is not uncommon for kids to take trips out of the country for things associated with school, sports, or sightseeing. Yes, going to Europe has become as common in the teen years as going to the prom or getting a car. It was not so for me as the fourth of six kids, born to a single parent, and on public assistance. In fact, I did not leave my hometown for more than 3 days until I was a junior in high school, and then it was to nearby Pittsburgh, PA, for a baseball tournament. All that changed my junior year, though, when one of my dear friend's dad took two other boys, his son, and me to (insert drum roll here)...Myrtle Beach, SC. When we arrived and I saw the ocean for the first time, I thought I had died and gone to heaven.

Nearly four decades have passed since I took that first "extended" trip out of New Martinsville, West Virginia, and it seems that I am still behind the majority of society. Just this summer, I took my first trip to Europe as part of my sabbatical from church. In between the time my wife first made those airline reservations and we landed safely back in the states, I've learned a great deal about money management and stewardship especially as it relates to visiting other countries.

Since getting to a country is usually the biggest cost, *keep track of those frequent flyer miles and educate yourself to when and how those miles can be used.* Once we decided that Europe would be our destination, we looked into how many frequent flyer miles we had and how much it would cost (of those miles) to get there. Next, we began looking into dates that the frequent flyer miles would allow us to travel and educating ourselves about the airlines restrictions as they relate to cashing in the frequent flyer miles. If you lack frequent flyer miles or choose to pay for the flight, go directly to the carrier's website to book. This commonly avoids any booking fees.

Be flexible and book early. We began planning nearly a year ahead of when we wanted to go. Since I was on sabbatical and my wife was "somewhat" flexible with her vacation time, we were not confined to leaving on a particular date and returning at a specific time. In turn, this gave us a great deal of latitude and helped with costs.

Order your passport early. Times to process passports vary from weeks to several weeks depending on the time of the year (spring and summer usually take longer). It's best to do it early and get it out of the way lest there is some last minute snag with processing.

Be sure to contact your bank and credit card institutions to tell them you are going out of the country for a while. It is commonplace for them to ask you where you'll be going and for how long so be ready with the information. Hey, they're being pro-

> *Hey, they're being pro-active and doing it for protection so lay-off!*

active and doing it for protection, so lay-off! The same day we arrived in England I charged fish and chips at a local restaurant. The next time I checked my e-mail I found a note from my bank asking if I had made the charge!

Ask your cell phone provider if they have any suggestions for you. Some providers offer loaner phones for a certain amount of time (say, 30 days). As well, be sure to look into rates. Many providers have packages that will cost you less than without the package. By all means, be sure to familiarize yourself with the package (how much for out-going and in-coming calls, text messages, etc). Once again, do your homework and negotiate!

Go to the website (or contact directly) of any hotels you plan to stay at during your visit and check for special rates. Those on-line discount websites that offer discount rates are nice, but they seldom have the best rates. Use

> **Consider a house exchange...we did it and it worked wonderfully!**

them to find an area where you want to stay, note the rates on that website for a particular hotel, and any amenities that the hotel may offer (free breakfast, shuttle service, free parking, etc). Then go directly to the website of the hotel you want to stay at or call them about rates. Beyond negotiating, ask about any discounts such as AAA, AARP, etc., and try not to accept the first rate offered! Chances are good that these last two moves (contacting the hotel directly and negotiating) will prove to be a "financially" good one!

Consider a house exchange...we did and it worked wonderfully! Maybe next to the cost of getting somewhere, the cost of staying there takes the biggest chunk out of the vacation dollar. Earlier this summer, my wife and I were able to stay at a home on the banks of the English Channel in southwest England for close to a month thanks to such an arrangement. In addition, we also got the use of a car as part of the exchange. However, the most fulfilling thing about such a course as this is that we got to immerse ourselves fully into the England culture. Yes, we went to London and did the tourist thing (Harrods, Big Ben, and the Tower of London) and we even made a side trip to France and Spain, but few things compare to spending an extended amount of time living in a small community whose ways of living are different from what we were accustomed to.

If you plan to leave a car for your "exchange" person to use, *contact your auto insurance carrier and explore your options regarding coverage.* As well, make sure all your legal stuff (living will, power of attorney, etc) are in the hands of a loved one...and don't forget your health insurance card. After all, you just never know what can happen so it's best to be ready.

If you decide to rent a car, *avoid renting at the airport*. Usually, those rental car places that are in-town and away from the airport are better deals. Many times, they will come and get you. *The same thing applies to hotels*; namely, a little further from the city-center can save big bucks! Caveat: is the hotel in a safe part of town and how far is it from local transportation such as the subway, a bus stop, or the train? BTW: If you plan to drive a lot, get a car with a GPS.

When possible, *use local transportation*. In addition to usually costing less, trains, buses, and local transportation allow a person to go place-to-place but with the added reward of seeing the sights minus having to drive around and fight traffic. Above all, the use of local transportation helps to orient you with your surroundings.

Upon arriving (if possible), *be sure to get a visitor's booklet or check the local newspaper for any special events, especially the free events*. Such a piece may contain a BOGO coupon, discount times, or special rates. By all means, don't forget to ask the locals or the people at the front desk about any discounts as well at restaurants, shows, etc.

As much as possible, *try to avoid using your credit card for cash advances.* If need be, make one stop and get as much as you think you'll need. This avoids those steep conversion fees from financial institutions. If you use an ATM, research which overseas banks have a working, sister agreement with your bank. Although you'll incur a fee for using them from your home bank and possibly the foreign bank (a flat fee plus a certain percent of the amount of the withdrawal), this may keep banking costs to a minimum. In addition, be sure to check with your bank about these fees before leaving. Finally, be sure to get a full print-out of all transactions that you conducted when you return to the states...just to make sure things are on the up-and-up.

> *Keep your receipts, especially if you charge or use your bank cards.*

It may sound strange and a little extreme, but *try to keep your receipts* (especially if you charge or use your bank cards). Not long after arriving back in the states, my wife got all the receipts (hotels, car rentals, etc.) along with the most recent bank statements and compared them. Did I mention that she was a CPA?

In closing, you may have noticed that I did not address one of the bigger issues...*how and what to pack*. I did this for two main reasons. For beginners, if a person wants to pack whatever they want, then let them do so. However, it may be wise to remind them that if a piece of luggage is overweight, it costs extra. More importantly, everybody tends to pack differently. Whereas some need to have a different outfit every day, I tend to pack less and wear the things that I did bring more (of course, I do change my "you-know-what" everyday). <u>This is how I look at it</u>: it doesn't bother me that I'm wearing the same thing I had on three days ago. After all, it's clean and I don't have to look at *me*...the person that I'm traveling with does!

Watch-out for These Store Tricks

The other day I went to the local grocery store to buy a gallon of milk. By the time I left, I had purchased a gallon of milk, two one-half gallons of ice cream (these were not for me, of course, but for my wife), a package of Colby cheese, and some Mt. Rainier cherries (these were for me). Instead of leaving with one bag, I left with three! Why? The answer is simple. First, I went to the store hungry...big mistake because everything looked good. Next, I fell into the store's magnetic pull because of the way the items were packaged and placed on the shelves. Lastly, I was drawn to buy the items that were BOGO (buy one, get one). Those rascals!

All of this leads me to say a few words about how stores "trick us" into buying things that we may not necessarily need and buying items we may not be able to afford. I fully realize that all of this is part of what is called marketing. However, if you want to become a better money manager and learn how to better handle your personal finances, you need to be aware of some little (subtle) things that stores do to make us leave with more than we came in with!

If possible, get a small plastic basket instead of a shopping cart. <u>Question:</u> what is the first thing that we see or are handed when we enter a grocery store? <u>Answer</u>: a shopping cart. Yes, it's automatic. The moment we enter a store we immediately begin looking for a shopping cart. The really smart stores have a person there to hand us one. Without thinking, we automatically take it and are on our way. In addition for something to lean-on when we see family and friends and begin talking, stores know that nobody wants to walk around with an empty cart. So, we put things in it even though we don't need these items! And the bigger the cart, the more we are drawn to fill it up.

The most expensive brands of things that have the most profit are found near in well-lighted, high traffic areas, usually near the entrance of the store. I'm not sure this entirely applies to grocery stores, but it sure does for department stores. Take jewelry for example. It seems that all roads lead there and all roads in-and-out of the store seem to intersect there. Again, it's by design. The same may (emphasis on "may") be said about grocery stores. I think of the place where I usually go grocery shopping. The fruit is just inside the door, the frozen stuff is next to that, and the meat and canned stuff is next to that. By the time I go though these departments, I'm nearly exhausted! And when I'm tired, I buy impulsively. My strategy is to go to the back of the store first and work my way forward. If I'm tired by the time I get to the frozen foods, the cold coming off the freezers of the ice cream aisle usually wakes me up. If not the cold, then definitely the lights of the produce department.

Watch out for narrow aisles that are full of people. Many stores are intentionally designed (and built) with narrow aisles because they make us more prone to stop as we allow others to go by. Once stopped, we begin looking around and it's then that we are more likely to buy something we don't need. The same thing applies to samples. It's a marketing fact: People who have to stop greatly increase their chances of buying. *Solution*: make a list and stick to it.

Similarly, try to avoid going down an aisle twice. Somehow, if I don't need a certain item the first time I go down an aisle, then I try not to be tempted a second time. One trip down the aisle and out! In like fashion, *be aware of those end-of-*

aisle things. It's almost as if the store is saying, "are you sure you don't need one of these for the kid's lunch boxes tomorrow or some of this for dinner tonight?" Again, keep moving and you'll be fine. We gave the store one chance for our business and we're not giving them a second one.

The most expensive items are at eye level. I try to practice a simple "eye" exercise when I go shopping...especially grocery shopping. After looking at things eye-level, I look up, I look down, and I look around. Try it the next time you're looking for items that are popular like potato chips or bread or cereal. The most recognized and the most brilliantly packaged items are at eye level. However, many times the store brands or the lesser recognized brands, packaged in less-spectacular bags, and costing less are usually found on the higher or lower shelves. Marketing people know that when people shop they start their search for items that are easily seen and easily reached. In addition to mixing the more expensive items with the less expensive items, grocery stores commonly place *the more expensive brands near the ends of the aisles.* Their strategy is clear; namely, shoppers slow down, if not stop completely, when they take a turn and move from one aisle to the next.

"On sale" items are usually placed in the middle or in close proximity to similar items. Let's say it's the day before Thanksgiving and you need some stuffing. So, you go to a particular grocery store because you know that store has stuffing mix on sale. When you get there, sure enough, there's the "on sale" stuffing mix. However, it's only after you get home do you realize that in addition to stuffing mix you've also

> *...we get confused over what's on sale and what's not on sale...*

purchased pumpkin pie mix, cranberry sauce, and a giant aluminum roasting pan because the one you have may not be big enough for that 22-pound turkey you purchased the day before! Whatever the case: we buy impulsively, we get confused over what's on sale and what's not on sale, or we buy more than we need because the items are shelved together, the result is the same. We overbuy! As well, this kind of marketing is not confined to grocery shopping. Yes, we can find this same approach to school and office supplies (paper that is on sale is placed next to pencils, pens and erasers that are not), sporting goods and accessories (golf balls may be on-sale but the golf glove, shoes, and tees are not) and everything in-between.

Stuff in those bargain bins aren't always a bargain. Marketing people know that we are drawn to things that say "bargain" or "sale" on them. The trouble is they may not always be that! Granted, the sign above the shelf or bin may say it, but many times when you take that particular item and compare it to the same item in another store, it will cost the same or even more.

The sale items, customer service booths, restrooms, and elevators are usually near the back of the store. When you need to return that tie the kids got you last year for Christmas (the one with the sequin reindeer on it), or the little one suddenly tells you that they need to go wee-wee, or you're ready to leave and do not want to risk taking the stroller down the escalator, wouldn't it be nice *not* to have to go through every department in the store to do so? No such luck! Stores put these amenities where they do for a reason: they do not want to miss one single opportunity to sell you something. Yes, on your way to the customer service booth to return that tie is men's clothing. As you go to the restroom, you'll probably pass the kids clothing. As for the elevator, it's commonly found near the housewares. Hey, if you need an elevator to take you from one floor to the next, why not buy some towels or sheets while you wait for it to arrive!

Finally, stores know people get bored standing in line to check-out, so *they line the path (I call it the gauntlet) to the cashier with expensive magazines, soda machines, and candy bars.* Once again, they want you to stop and look around. If you do this, then they can increase their

> *... I call it the gauntlet*

chances of you buying something. Similarly, *stores have a way of always being short of cashiers.* Am I right? Again, they want you to stop, because if you stop then they have you right where they want you. When I am ready to check out, I always look at the size of the line that's ahead of me. If it's more than 3 people and they have a lot of things, I always go to the store office and ask the manager if they can open another line. Amazingly, someone is always there in a few moments! It's almost as if they know we know what they're doing and they jump into action.

X-tra Cash

Until I hit the Powerball lottery (and it should be any day now considering how much I play), I am constantly on the look-out for how to make my dollars go further. Granted, it helps to use what's left-over from the expense side to supplement the income side, but there are times when I need a little more to make ends meets.

In this chapter, I share some (legal) ways that will bring you some extra cash. Some of these are ones that I have actually done and some are ways that others around me have done to raise some extra cash. Either way, these are suggestions not hard fast-rules. Any extra income should be put toward reducing or eliminating any outstanding debt.

By the way, I really don't play the Powerball lottery that much...Wednesday and Saturday only...when I remember! As for my numbers, I'll tell you my system after I win!

Have a yard sale. In addition to reducing the amount of clutter in your home, this is a sure-fire way to raise some extra cash. After all, "one man's treasure is another man's trash" (or vice-versa). <u>Some pointers</u>: (a) be sure to advertise early and as often as possible (get the dates and location of your sale into as many free literature pieces as possible and be sure that the date, time, and address are clearly marked on the information); (b) keep the price of your items reasonable (remember, it's a yard sale and not a sale at Sotheby's); (c) consider teaming-up with some neighbors and doing stations (you do furniture, the next neighbor does baby clothes, the next neighbor does sporting goods, and so on). If you really want to do it up right, you have a map ready for your customers that shows them which neighbor is selling which things); (d) send your kids and your spouse away during the sale (if the kids insist on staying, then let them run a food stand); (e) treat each customer like they are royalty; (f) be ready to have a "fire sale" at the close of sale hours (everything a customer can fit into one grocery bag for $5.00); (g) and be ready to haggle (but remember, always let your customer win…remember, you need their money).

Sell your old textbooks. Determine which ones you want to keep and which ones you want to sell at the local secondhand bookstore or on-line.

Keep the classics because they will never go out of style. However, get rid of any that you think are taking-up space and collecting dust.

Give blood. Don't laugh...it helped with some of my bills while I was in graduate school at West Virginia University and it even gave me some extra spending money! I'm not sure what blood banks are paying now for a pint, but I suggest this only as a last resort for adults. If you're in college, then do it for the experience of meeting some "new and interesting people."

> *...do it for the experience of meeting some "new and interesting people."*

Sign-up to be a secret shopper. I've done this and it's no big a deal. You go "undercover" to a store or restaurant and then you rate how they do things (customer service, the quality of the food, etc). Then, you pass that information on to the big boys in corporate. It's another of those "win-win situations"...you get some cash and the store or restaurant learns how to do things better.

Teach or tutor. Listen-up current college students, former teachers, and anyone that knows a particular subject area: this is a gold mine! Granted, I've never tutored, but I have paid someone to tutor my kids in chemistry and math. Subsequently, I know how much a tutor makes per hour, and believe me it's a good rate. As for teaching, I do it as a sideline to my "real" job. Although the money is not that much (I teach at a small private college), the position keeps me up-to-date with current research and scholasticism and that is compensation in itself.

Adjust your withholding tax. This is one of those areas that you really need to talk to someone other than me...like a CPA or the person that does your taxes. <u>Here's how I look at it</u>: if you got a refund on your taxes last year, then you overpaid. And if you overpaid, then that money has sat in Uncle Sam's pocket for the last year and not yours! More, Uncle Sam didn't pay interest on the money he was "holding" for you.

Don't let your side job interfere with your fulltime job.

Make your hobby work for you. If you enjoy photography, then get on the list to do some weddings. If you like to cook, then consider doing some catering. If you know how to do taxes, then go and talk to people at some of these income tax preparation places. If you know the difference between a USB port and a port wine cheese, then consider doing computer work on the side. <u>One caveat</u>: don't let your side job interfere with you full-time job.

Selling unwanted gold, selling on E-Bay or Craigslist, home businesses, clinical trials, or pizza delivery. I don't know much about some of these, so I'll simply say "silence is golden!" As for the others, weigh the cost (financial, emotional, and physical) of selling the stuff versus the benefits.

Yahoo for Free Entertainment and Such

Among those that know me, it is a well-known fact that if there's something free out there...I'll find it! Granted, few things are free, but there are a great number of things that cost next to nothing. In this chapter, I want to share with you some of the things you can do that are free or next-to-nothing. In addition, I've listed some things that you will want to check-out that are easy on the wallet. For example...

The local *library* has a treasure chest of items for free including books and magazines, movies on DVD, and newspapers from around the world.

Remember to "comb" the local newspaper and other sources with an eye toward finding out when movie theaters, zoos, and other public places offer *discount days*.

If you have a *computer*, freebies are just as numerous. Go on-line to set-up a free e-mail account (gmail.com, Yahoo.com, or hotmail.com), download music, watch re-runs of your favorite TV show or movie, or even hear a favorite radio station. While you're at it, you may also want to download free software for your computer to guard against spyware and viruses.

As well, you are also entitled to one *free credit report* a year from each of the three main credit bureaus (Trans Union, Experian, and Equifax). Regardless of the way you choose to go, calling 1-877-322-8228, going to www.annualcredit report.com, or by simply mailing the completed form, it's free and well-worth the effort.

A *home-energy check* by your local utilities provider is a great way to receive an analysis of not only how much energy and water consumption you use but also ways to reduce your energy bill. The free inspection reviews your home's insulation, cooling and heating systems, and overall efficiency.

Interested in taking a *free college or university course* on-line from some of the top schools in the nation, including MIT, Johns Hopkins University, and Harvard Law School, it's possible. Granted, you won't get credit toward a college degree, but you can pursue an interest or sharpen your skills thanks to the course materials being posted on the Internet.

Free legal and medical advice is found all over the web. However, "caveat emptor."

On select nights through the week, *kids eat free* at Denny's, Lone Star Steakhouse, Captain D's, and several other restaurants with a paying adult. As well, many of the Denny's restaurants give a person a free meal on their birthday! Finally, more and more fast food restaurants are giving out coupons for free food if a person takes a simple survey (i.e. Burger King, Arby's, etc).

Before you go to your local pharmacist to get that prescription filled from your doctor, *ask if the doctor has any free samples.*

With free software from Skype, a person can *chat free* via computer with family and friends. While you won't pay a single dime for any call to another Skype user, you can call non-Skype users land lines for about $3.00 a month.

Although they are becoming fewer and fewer, a good place for *free food* is a place that offers happy hour. Granted, you may have to buy something to drink, but it can be something as inexpensive as a soda.

Many times, university dental, beauty, and trade schools offer *free or reduced services* for individuals. The examination and services will be performed by "students in training" but a professional is nearby to oversee them.

A person can get *free clothes drying* by simply hanging them out on a sunny day and letting Mother Nature do the drying. The amount of money saved can add up to be hundreds of dollars yearly.

> *The amount of money saved can add up to be hundreds of dollars yearly.*

If you're three-score or older, then you qualify to get your *tax returns* done for free. The best place to start here is the IRS website.

Zilch

With this concluding chapter, it seems we have come full circle. In the preceding chapters, I have shared with you some ways to cut everyday expenses such as paying bills through EFT, negotiating, and what to watch-out for when grocery shopping. However, this work would not be complete if I failed to mention the things in this life that I absolutely, positively refuse to pay for. In other words, there are some things in this world that I refuse to pay for...zero, nothing, zilch. Again, it's not that I'm cheap, but frugal. That list...

Annual fee for a credit card. Don't get me started on this credit card thing again! One would think that late payment fees are enough to keep the credit card institutions solvent, but maybe not. Then again, maybe that's why they invented annual fees.

Banking fees, especially a fee to use an ATM. Granted, banks should get some money for us using the machines. But for the owner of that ATM to charge us a fee and our own bank to charge us a fee makes me shake my head. Think about it like this: how much are we being charged for convenience?

Checking e-mail when I'm out of town or away from my computer. Again, go to the closest public library and do it for free.

Dessert at a restaurant. For about the same cost that you get one scoop of that Rocky Road ice cream at a restaurant you can get a half-gallon of ice cream at the local grocery store.

Event (sports or otherwise) parking. In addition to not having to pay some exorbitant fee to park, I refuse to pay for event parking especially when I can park my car for free a few blocks away, hop on a bus for free, and usually be at the event with money in my pocket, some exercise, and a great deal less stress.

> *...I refuse to pay for event parking especially when I can park for free a few blocks away...*

Food at sporting events. Like the real estate around a sporting event, have you noticed lately how much food costs increase once you get close or inside a professional sporting event? Miraculously, food that you can buy on the outside for $4.00 costs you suddenly $7.00 or $8.00 on the inside. It's the same food! In fact, I would bet that much of the food sold in a stadium is prepared outside the stadium. I guess the cost to transport the food into the stadium is the reason for the cost increase.

Golf balls. The last time I bought golf balls (which was about 3 years ago) they cost anywhere from $5.00 to $10.00 for a sleeve (box of three). If you want to pay next-to-nothing for golf balls, then follow my lead and go walking around the golf course just before dusk. My bet is that you'll find enough golf balls to make it through the next time you play golf.

Hot or cold food at the airport. See "food at sporting events" and you can get my drift!

Ice (bags). Why buy bags of ice at some exorbitant price when you can have all the ice you want for free with some minor planning ahead. A week or so before you plan that trip to the beach, dump all the ice you have in your ice cube trays (no, I don't have an ice maker...and yes, I still use trays) into a plastic freezer bag, stick that bag of ice in the freezer, refill the trays, wait a few hours, and repeat. Better yet, freeze bottles of water. This way you can kill two birds with one stone: ice and cold water!

Junk at yard sales. My reasoning is clear: if I don't already have it, then I probably don't need it.

Kitchen/refrigerator magnets. These things are as common as oxygen.

Lawn care, painting and other small things around the house. In other words, I refuse to pay for the things that I can do myself. More, it's good exercise and gives me another skill.

Movies. Libraries have DVD's or movies that have been donated by their patrons. If that's not satisfying enough, then I break out my computer and watch reruns of my favorite TV shows and movies on-line.

Newspapers and magazines. Go to the library.

Overdue things. Why? I put the due date on the calendar. This works especially well for mortgage payments, when a book that I checked-out from the library is due, and when payments are due for "irregular" things such driver's license renewal.

Packing and shipping. Remember: negotiate, negotiate, negotiate.

Quick fix-up's around the house. When I need to do a small project around the house I go to the local home improvement store and attend a workshop.

Rental car insurance. More times than none, my regular auto insurance covers it.

Student financial aid forms. Most standard forms are free including the most important one: the FAFSA.

Tea, coffee, and soft drinks at a restaurant. Next to certain items, drinks have the highest mark-ups. Me? I drink water, straight-up…with a lemon.

Undercoating on an automobile. Either it's already done at the factory, it doesn't need to be done, or else I can do it.

Virus protection. You guessed it…on-line, and many of them are free.

Water (bottled). Like a parking lot near a sports

venue and the food sold within, the price for bottled water is amazing. Me? If I buy a bottle, I save the bottle and simply refill it with tap water. It serves the same purpose and costs pennies.

X-tra costs associated with getting an item shipped to me. Watch for the small print, spend a certain amount, or simply ask for it.

Yard work. That's why we have kids, right?

Yard work... that's why we have kids, right?

Zip lock bags. Here the sky's the limit. If you simply want to put something in a plastic bag, consider using the plastic that the loaf of bread came in, or how about a plastic grocery bag.

Prologue

That's it...pretty much all this particular minister knows about saving money, becoming a better money-manager, and a good steward of what money we already have. And lest you be one of those people that goes immediately to the back of the book because you don't have time to read what's between the covers, let me recap for you 26 of what I feel are the biggest, single items a person can do to trim their expenses. In keeping with the theme of this book, they're listed A thru Z.

A – Automobile   All the stars need to line-up (trade-in, financing, options, etc) before you go buying a car.

B – Banking   Banking on-line, especially paying bills, saves big bucks.

C – Coupons   Compare shop, use coupons, and redeem coupons wisely (like at stores that double and triple coupons).

D – Debit/   Don't use your credit card for everyday things   unless that card gives you cash back or airline miles.

E – Education   Enroll your kids in a (state) 529 plan.

F – Flying   Flexibility (when to purchase, when to fly, etc) has its rewards.

G – Grocery   Remember, generic, generic, generic.

H – Health/gym clubs How far is the club from where you live or work?

I – Insurance   If you compare car rates every 6 months, you may save hundreds of dollars annually.

J – Jargon   Just know what your insurance terms mean.

K – Kids   Kids should not lend-out their car to their friends.

L – Legal   Living wills need to be well-thought out, signed, and witnessed.

M – Miscellaneous   Maintain enough in savings to cover 6 months of regular, everyday expenses.

N – Negotiate   Negotiating is best when it's done at the right time and with the right attitude.

O – Outside eating   Order an appetizer as a meal and drink water.

P – Property   Pay January mortgage payment and yearly property taxes in December of the preceding year.

Q – Quick and easy things   Things need to be purchased quickly in the off-season in order to get the best price.

R – Road trips   State rest stops are a great place to get discount books for attractions, hotel rooms, etc.

S – Service stations   Stay out of the store and pay for your gas at the pump.

T – Telephone   Two phones (a cell phone and a landline) are a no-no.

U – Utilities   Understand that insulating the attic can save on your utility/energy bill.

V – Visiting foreign countries   Visiting the website of a hotel, airline, or car rental company can save money.

W – Watch-out   Walking down a crowded store aisle or going down an aisle a second time will cost you.

X – Xtra   X-tra jobs should never interfere with your primary/full-time job.

Y – Yahoo for free things   You can always check your e-mail while you're doing things on the road at a public library for free.

Z – Zilch   Zero is what you should pay for event parking.

In closing, I want to share with you some thoughts about what may be the most important aspect in this whole process of stewardship,

> *I promise...*
> *these are*
> *my last few*
> *words.*

money management, and personal finance. That aspect: preparing...and sticking to...a budget. With that, some final thoughts to keep in mind as you go about this process. I promise these are my last few words!

Learn the difference between wants and needs. I am convinced that the key to good stewardship and personal finance is being able to distinguish between the two. The things like food, a roof over our heads, and a reliable means to get from one place to the other are *needs*. Conversely, getting a new pair of Crocs just because the company came out with a new color, buying delivered pizza when you can get the same for about half the price at the local grocery store, and purchasing new furniture for the "man-cave" when worn will do just as good I classify as "wants."

Make and keep a list of income and what you spend your money on. In other words, track your spending. Beyond telling you how you're spending your money...on wants or needs...tracking your spending says a great deal about your spending habits. Best of all, tracking spending reduces the chance of us missing a payment and suffering the consequences connected with it.

Prioritize. This is a no brainer! Mortgage (rent), utilities, groceries, and insurance should be at the top. And don't forget about your regular offering to church. Do as I do and make this last aspect as commonplace as the car payment.

Make regular adjustments and re-organize as

needed. If after tracking your spending for several months you notice that groceries are getting too much of the lion's share, then stop and consider why. Impulsive buying? Not doing your homework and shopping the sales? Do you have enough food in your refrigerator or pantry to feed an army? Are you throwing out more and more food because it goes bad? If so, then try reducing your food budget.

Be disciplined. Becoming a good steward and money manager takes time. My mother didn't do it overnight, I didn't do it over night, and neither can you. So, begin small and build from there. Above all, be patient…but be persistent.

Begin with a few of the suggestions and increase from there. As I have stated all along in this work, use what you want and leave the rest! Remember, small things add up.

Enjoy what you work so hard for! I am. After all, life is meant to be enjoyed and not merely endured.

Dr. Michael F. Price
Washington/Cary, NC
Summer, 2009